CONTENTS

THE LIFE OF ST. PAUL

THE LIFE
OF ST. PAUL

James Stalker

Academie
Books from Zondervan
Publishing House

1415 Lake Drive, S.E., Grand Rapids, Michigan 49506

THE LIFE OF ST. PAUL
Copyright © 1983 by The Zondervan Corporation
Grand Rapids, Michigan

ACADEMIE BOOKS is an imprint of Zondervan Publishing House,
1415 Lake Drive, S.E., Grand Rapids, Michigan 49506

Library of Congress Cataloging in Publication Data

Stalker, James, 1848–1927.
    The life of St. Paul.

    1. Paul, the Apostle, Saint. 2. Christian saints—
Turkey—Tarsus—Biography. 3. Bible. N.T.—Biography.
I. Title. II Title: The life of St. Paul.
BS2505.S7   1983   225.9′24 [B]   83-19769
ISBN 0-310-44181-1

Printed in the United States of America

83 84 85 86 87 88 / 10 9 8 7 6 5 4 3 2 1

FOREWORD
By WILBERT W. WHITE, D.D.

When asked to write a Foreword to Dr. Stalker's *Life of St. Paul,* I thought of two things: first; the impression I had received from a sermon that I heard Dr. Stalker preach a good many years ago in his own pulpit in Glasgow, Scotland, and secondly, the honor conferred in this privilege of writing a Foreword to one of Dr. Stalker's books.

I felt sure before even glancing at the pages that I should be pleased and profited by their perusal.

The first thing that I did was to glance over the pages for the headings of chapters and the summaries of paragraphs. I found the arrangement admirable, and would advise those into whose hands this fine volume may come to follow this plan.

The only sentence apart from the headings that I read in the aforesaid preview was the last one in Chapter 10, and that because the closing words, "the best of friends," especially arrested my attention.

I wondered before I read this sentence if the author was saying of Paul that he was going out of the world to the One who had been to him the best of friends. From this you may gather—what you like. Only I felt sure before reading the pages that Dr. Stalker would interpret Paul in a manner such as I could enthusiastically approve.

And now having read the volume I heartily commend it. It is the best brief life of Paul of which I know.

Before reading the book I said to myself, I shall put down what I think the writer will make the heart of the secret of Paul. It was this: The key to Paul's efficiency was his wholehearted persistent loyalty to Christ, his Savior and Friend. He was not disobedient to the heavenly vision. He stood fast in the liberty wherewith Christ set him free. He was three things all stated in one verse, and put thus: "I am crucified with Christ—Christ liveth in me—I live in faith."

Here are some, a very few of many striking, true thoughts presented by Dr. Stalker:

"Paul was the interpreter of Christ, saying what Christ Himself would have said under the circumstances."

"Paul's entire theology was nothing but the explication of his own conversion."

"In bringing Paul West, Providence gave to Europe a blessed priority, and the fate of our continent was decided, when Paul crossed the Aegean."

"A secret of Paul's success was his sense of having a mission and his freedom alike from the bondage of bigotry and the bondage of liberty."

A writer recently gave me this thought about Paul: "What makes St. Paul so interesting is his conception of the dimensions of life."

Back to Christ? Yes, the whole world needs it, but the way to get back to Christ is through the apostolic interpretation of Christ in words and life. This is the only way, and Dr. Stalker's book is a great help in this direction.

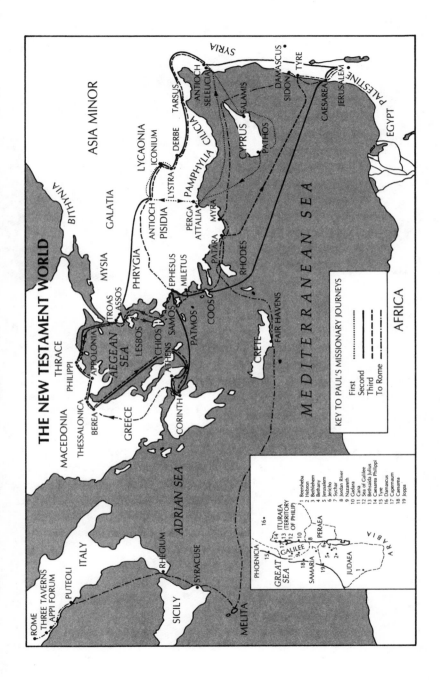

THE NEW TESTAMENT WORLD

ASIA MINOR

BITHYNIA

THRACE

MACEDONIA

PHILIPPI

THESSALONICA

APPOLONIA

BEREA

GREECE

ATHENS

CORINTH

ITALY

ROME
THREE TAVERNS
APPI FORUM
PUTEOLI

RHEGIUM

SICILY

SYRACUSE

MELITA

ADRIAN SEA

M E D I T E R R A N E A N   S E A

AFRICA

MYSIA

GALATIA

PHRYGIA

TROAS
ASSOS

LESBOS

CHIOS

SAMOS

AEGEAN SEA

PATMOS

EPHESUS

MILETUS

COOS

CRETE

FAIR HAVENS

RHODES

PATARA

MYRA

ATTALIA

PERGA

PAMPHYLIA

PISIDIA

ANTIOCH

LYCAONIA

ICONIUM

DERBE

LYSTRA

CILICIA

TARSUS

ANTIOCH
SELEUCIA

CYPRUS

SALAMIS

PAPHOS

SYRIA

DAMASCUS

SIDON

TYRE

CAESAREA

JERUSALEM

PALESTINE

EGYPT

KEY TO PAUL'S MISSIONARY JOURNEYS

First
Second
Third
To Rome

PHOENICIA

GREAT
SEA

SAMARIA

JUDAEA

GALILEE

PERAEA

ITURAEA
(TERRITORY
OF PHILIP)

ARABIA

1 Beersheba
2 Hebron
3 Bethlehem
4 Bethany
5 Jerusalem
6 Jericho
7 Sychar
8 Jordan River
9 Nazareth
10 Gadara
11 Cana
12 Sea of Galilee
13 Bethsaida Julius
14 Caesarea Philippi
15 Tyre
16 Damascus
17 Capernaum
18 Caesarea
19 Joppa

1

HIS PLACE IN HISTORY

THE MAN FOR THE TIME

1. There are some men whose lives it is impossible to study without receiving the impression that they were expressly sent into the world to do a work required by the juncture of history on which they fell. The story of the Reformation, for example, cannot be read by a devout mind without wondering at the providence by which such great men as Luther, Zwingli, Calvin, and Knox were simultaneously raised up in different parts of Europe to break the yoke of the papacy and republish the gospel of grace. When the Evangelical Revival, after blessing England, was about to break into Scotland and end the dreary reign of Moderatism, there was raised up in Thomas Chalmers a mind of such capacity as completely to absorb the new movement into itself, and of such sympathy and influence as to diffuse it to every corner of his native land.

2. This impression is produced by no life more than by that of the apostle Paul. He was given to Christianity when it was in its most rudimentary beginnings. It was

not, indeed, feeble, nor can any mortal man be spoken of as indispensable to it; for it contained within itself the vigor of a divine and immortal existence, which could not but have unfolded itself in the course of time. But, if we recognize that God makes use of means that commend themselves even to our eyes as suited to the ends He has in view, then we must say that the Christian movement at the moment when Paul appeared on the stage was in the utmost need of a man of extraordinary endowments, who, becoming possessed with its genius, should incorporate it with the general history of the world; and in Paul it found the man it needed.

A TYPE OF CHRISTIAN CHARACTER

3. Christianity produced in Paul an incomparable type of Christian character. It already, indeed, possessed the perfect model of human character in the person of its Founder. But our Lord was not as other men, because from the beginning He had no sinful imperfection to struggle with; and Christianity still needed to show what it could make of imperfect human nature. Paul supplied the opportunity of exhibiting this. He was naturally of immense mental stature and force. He would have been a remarkable man even if he had never become a Christian. The other apostles would have lived and died in the obscurity of Galilee if they had not been lifted into prominence by the Christian movement; but the name of Saul of Tarsus would have been remembered still in some character or other even if Christianity had never existed. Christianity got the opportunity in him of showing to the world the whole force it contained. Paul was aware of this himself, though he expressed it with perfect modesty, when he said, "For this cause I obtained mercy, that in me first Jesus Christ might shew forth all longsuffering for a pattern to them which should hereafter believe on him to life everlasting."

4. His conversion proved the power of Christianity to overcome the strongest prejudices and to stamp its own type on a large nature by a revolution both instantaneous and permanent. Paul's was a personality so strong and original that no other man could have been less expected to sink himself in another; but, from the moment when he came into contact with Christ, he was so overmastered with His influence that he later never had any other desire than to be the mere echo and reflection of Him to the world.

But, if Christianity showed its strength in making so complete a conquest of Paul, it showed its worth no less in the kind of man it made of him when he had given himself up to its influence. It satisfied the needs of a peculiarly hungry nature, and never to the close of his life did he betray the slightest sense that this satisfaction was abating. His constitution was originally compounded of fine materials, but the spirit of Christ, passing into these, raised them to a pitch of excellence altogether unique.

Nor was it ever doubtful either to himself or to others that it was the influence of Christ that made him what he was. The truest motto for his life would be his own saying, "I live, yet not I, but Christ liveth in me." Indeed, so perfectly was Christ formed in him that we can now study Christ's character in his, and beginners may perhaps learn even more of Christ from studying Paul's life than from studying Christ's own. In Christ Himself there was a blending and softening of all the excellences that makes His greatness elude the glance of the beginner, just as the very perfection of Raphael's painting makes it disappointing to an untrained eye; whereas in Paul a few of the greatest elements of Christian character were exhibited with a decisiveness that no one can mistake.

A GREAT THINKER

5. Christianity obtained in Paul, secondly, a great thinker. This it especially needed in Paul's day. Christ had departed from the world, and those whom He had left to represent Him were unlettered fishermen and, for the most part, men of no intellectual mark. In one sense this fact reflects a peculiar glory about Christianity, for it shows that it did not owe its place as one of the great influences of the world to the abilities of its human representatives: not by might nor by power, but by the Spirit of God, was Christianity established in the earth. Yet, as we look back now, we can clearly see how essential it was that an apostle of a different stamp and training should arise.

6. Christ had manifested the glory of the Father once for all and completed His atoning work. But this was not enough. It was necessary that the meaning of His appearance should be explained to the world. Who was He who had been here? What precisely was it He had done? To these questions the original apostles could give brief popular answers; but none of them had the intellectual reach or the educational training necessary to put the answers into a form to satisfy the intellect of the world. It is not essential to salvation to be able to answer such questions with scientific accuracy, happily. There are tens of thousands who know and believe that Jesus was the Son of God and died to take away sin and, trusting Him as their Savior, are purified by faith, but who could not explain these statements at any length without falling into mistakes in almost every sentence. Yet, if Christianity was to make an intellectual as well as a moral conquest of the world, it was necessary for the church to have accurately explained to her the full glory of her Lord and the meaning of His saving work.

Of course Jesus Himself had in His mind a comprehension both of what He was and of what He was doing, which was as luminous as the sun. But it was one of the most pathetic aspects of His earthly ministry that He could not tell all His mind to His followers. They were not able to bear it; they were too rude and limited to take it in. He had to carry His deepest thoughts out of the world with Him unuttered, trusting with a sublime faith that the Holy Spirit would lead His church to grasp them in the course of its subsequent development. Even what He did utter was imperfectly understood.

There was one mind, it is true, in the original apostolic circle of the finest quality and that was capable of soaring into the rarest altitudes of speculation. The words of Christ sank into the mind of John and, after lying there for half a century, grew up into the wonderful forms we inherit in his Gospel and Epistles. But even the mind of John was not equal to the exigency of the church; it was too fine, mystical, unusual. His thoughts to this day remain the property only of the few finest minds. There was needed a thinker of broader and more massive make to sketch the first outlines of Christian doctrine; and he was found in Paul.

7. Paul was a born thinker. His mind was of majestic breadth and force. It was restlessly busy, never able to leave any object with which it had to deal until it had pursued it back to its remotest causes and forward into all its consequences. It was not enough for him to know that Christ was the Son of God: he had to unfold this statement into its elements and understand precisely what it meant. It was not enough for him to believe that Christ died for sin: he had to go farther and inquire why it was necessary that he should do so and how His death took sin away.

But not only did he have from nature this speculative gift: his talent was trained by education. The other apostles were unlettered men; but he enjoyed the fullest scholastic advantages of the period. In the rabbinical school he learned how to arrange and state and defend his ideas. We have the result of all this in his Epistles, which contain the best explanation of Christianity possessed by the world. The right way to look at them is to regard them as the continuation of Christ's own teaching. They contain the thoughts that Christ carried away from the earth with Him unuttered. Of course Jesus would have stated them differently and far better. Paul's thoughts have everywhere the coloring of his own mental peculiarities. But the substance of them is what Christ's must have been if He had Himself given them expression.

8. There was one great subject especially that Christ had to leave unexplained—His own death. He could not explain it before it had taken place. This became the leading topic of Paul's thinking—to show why it was needed and what were its blessed results. But there was no aspect of the appearance of Christ into which his restlessly inquiring mind did not penetrate. His thirteen Epistles, when arranged in chronological order, show that his mind was constantly getting deeper and deeper into the subject. The progress of his thinking was determined partly by the natural progress of his own advance in the knowledge of Christ, for he always wrote out of his own experience; and partly by the various forms of error that he had at successive periods encountered, and which became a providential means of stimulating and developing his apprehension of the truth, just as ever since in the Christian church the rise of error has been the means of calling forth the clearest statements of doctrine. The ruling impulse, however, of his thinking, as of his life, was ever Christ, and it was his lifelong devotion to this exhaustless theme that made him the thinker of Christianity.

THE MISSIONARY TO THE GENTILES

9. Christianity can claim in Paul, thirdly, the missionary to the Gentiles. It is rare to find the highest

speculative power united with great practical activity; but these were united in him. He was not only the church's greatest thinker, but also the most important worker she has ever possessed. We have been considering the speculative task that was awaiting him when he joined the Christian community; but there was a no less stupendous practical task awaiting him too. This was the evangelization of the gentile world.

10. One of the great objects of the appearance of Christ was to break down the wall of separation between Jew and Gentile and make the blessings of salvation the property of all men, without distinction of race or language. But He was not Himself permitted to carry this change into practical realization. It was one of the strange limitations of His earthly life that He was sent only to the lost sheep of the house of Israel. It can easily be imagined how congenial a task it would have been to His intensely human heart to carry the gospel beyond the limits of Palestine and make it known to nation after nation; and—if it is not too bold to say so—this would certainly have been His chosen career, had He been spared. But He died at an early age and had to leave this task to His followers.

11. Before the appearance of Paul on the scene, the execution of this task had been begun. Jewish prejudice had been partially broken down, the universal character of Christianity had been in some measure realized, and Peter had admitted the first Gentiles into the church by baptism. But none of the original apostles was equal to the emergency. None of them was large-minded enough to grasp the idea of the perfect equality of Jew and Gentile and apply it without flinching in all its practical consequences; and none of them had the combination of gifts necessary to attempt the conversion of the gentile world on a large scale. They were Galilean fishermen, fit enough to teach and preach within the bounds of their native Palestine. But beyond Palestine lay the great world of Greece and Rome—the world of vast populations, of power and culture, of pleasure and business. It needed a man of unlimited versatility, of education, of immense human sympathy and breadth, to go out there with the gospel message—a man who could not only be a Jew to the Jews, but a Greek to the Greeks, a Roman to the Romans, a barbarian to the barbarians—a man who could encounter not only rabbis in their synagogues, but proud magistrates in their courts and philosophers in the haunts of learning—a man who could face travel by land and by sea, who could exhibit presence of mind in every variety of circumstances, and would be cowed by no difficulties. No man of this size belonged to the original apostolic circle; but Christianity needed such a person, and he was found in Paul.

12. Originally attached more strictly than any of the other apostles to the peculiarities and prejudices of Jewish exclusiveness, Paul cut his way out of the jungle of these prepossessions, accepted the equality of all men in Christ, and applied this principle relentlessly in all its issues. He gave his heart to the gentile mission, and the history of his life is the history of how true he was to his vocation. There was never such singleness of eye or wholeness of heart. There was never such superhuman and untiring energy. There was never such an accumulation of difficulties victoriously met and of sufferings cheerfully borne for any cause. In him Jesus Christ went forth to evangelize the world, making use of his hands and feet, his tongue and brain and heart, for doing the work that in His own bodily presence He had not been permitted by the limits of His mission to accomplish.

2

HIS UNCONSCIOUS PREPARATION FOR HIS WORK

GOD'S PLAN

13. Persons whose conversion takes place after they are grown up are accustomed to looking back on the period of their life that has preceded this event with sorrow and shame and wishing that an obliterating hand might blot the record of it out of existence. Paul felt this sentiment strongly: to the end of his days he was haunted by the specters of his lost years, and would say that he was the least of all the apostles, who was not worthy to be called an apostle, because he had persecuted the church of

God. But these somber sentiments are only partially justifiable. God's purposes are very deep, and even in those who do not know Him He may be sowing seeds that will only ripen and bear fruit long after their godless career is over. Paul would never have been the man he became or have done the work he did, if he had not, in the years preceding his conversion, gone through a course of preparation designed to fit him for his subsequent career. He did not know what he was being prepared for; his own intentions about his future were different from God's; but there is a divinity that shapes our ends, and it was making him a polished shaft for God's quiver, though he did not know it.

BIRTH AND BIRTHPLACE

14. The date of Paul's birth is not exactly known, but it can be settled with a closeness of approximation that is sufficient for practical purposes. When in the year A.D. 33 those who stoned Stephen laid down their clothes at Paul's feet, he was "a young man." This term has, indeed, in Greek as much latitude as in English, and may indicate any age from something under twenty to something over thirty. In this case it probably touched the latter rather than the former limit; for there is reason to believe that at this time, or very soon after, he was a member of the Sanhedrin—an office that no one could hold who was under thirty years of age—and the commission he received from the Sanhedrin immediately afterward to persecute the Christians would scarcely have been entrusted to a very young man. About thirty years after playing this sad part in Stephen's murder, in the year A.D. 62, he was lying in a prison in Rome awaiting sentence of death for the same cause for which Stephen had suffered, and, writing one of the last of his Epistles, that to Philemon, he called himself an old man. This term also is one of great latitude, and a man who had gone through so many hardships might well be old before his time; yet he could scarcely have taken the name of "Paul the aged" before sixty years of age.

These calculations lead us to the conclusion that he was born about the same time as Jesus. When the boy Jesus was playing in the streets of Nazareth, the boy Paul was playing in the streets of his native town, on the other side of the ridges of Lebanon. They seemed likely to have totally diverse careers. Yet, by the mysterious arrangement of Providence, these two lives, like streams flowing from opposite watersheds, were one day, as a river and tributary, to mingle together.

15. The place of his birth was Tarsus, the capital of the province of Cilicia, in the southeast of Asia Minor. It stood a few miles from the coast, in the midst of a fertile plain, and was built on both banks of the river Cydnus, which descended to it from the neighboring Taurus Mountains, on the snowy peaks of which the inhabitants of the town were accustomed, on summer evenings, to watch from the flat roofs of their houses the glow of the sunset. Not far above the town the river poured over the rocks in a vast cataract, but below this it became navigable, and within the town its banks were lined with wharves, on which were piled the merchandise of many countries, while sailors and merchants, dressed in the costumes and speaking the languages of different races, were constantly to be seen in the streets. The town enjoyed an extensive trade in timber, with which the province abounded, and in the long fine hair of the goats kept by the thousands on the neighboring mountains. This hair was made into a coarse kind of cloth and manufactured into various articles, among them tents, such as Paul was later employed in sewing, formed an extensive article of merchandise all along the shores of the Mediterranean. Tarsus was also the center of a large transport trade, for behind the town a famous pass, called the Cilician Gates, led up through the mountains to the central countries of Asia Minor; and Tarsus was the depot to which the products of these countries were brought down, to be distributed over the East and the West.

The inhabitants of the city were numerous and wealthy. The majority of them were native Cilicians, but the wealthiest merchants were Greeks. The province was under the sway of the Romans, the signs of whose sovereignty were not absent from the capital, although Tarsus itself enjoyed the privilege of self-government. The number and variety of the inhabitants were still further increased by the fact that, like the city of Glasgow, Tarsus was not only a center of commerce, but also a seat of learning. It was one of the three principal university cities of the period, the other two being Athens and Alexandria; and it was said to surpass its rivals in intellectual eminence. Students from many countries were to be seen in its streets, a sight that could not but awaken in youthful minds thoughts about the value and the aims of learning.

16. Who does not see how fit a place this was for the apostle to the gentiles to be born in? As he grew older, he was unconsciously being prepared to encounter men of every class and race, to sympathize with human nature in all its varieties, and to look with tolerance on the most diverse habits and customs. Later in his life he was always a lover of cities. Whereas his Master avoided Jerusalem and loved to teach on the mountainside or the shore of the lake, Paul was constantly moving from one great city to another. Antioch, Ephesus, Athens, Corinth, Rome, the capitals of the ancient world, were the scenes of his activity. The words of Jesus are suggestive of the country, and teem with pictures of its still beauty or homely toil—the lilies of the field, the sheep following the shepherd, the sower in the furrow, the fishermen drawing their nets; but the language of Paul is impregnated with the atmosphere of the city and is alive with the tramp and hurry of the streets. His imagery is borrowed from scenes of human energy and monuments of cultivated life—the soldier in full armor, the athlete in the arena, the building of houses and temples, the triumphal procession of the victorious general. So lasting are the associations of the boy in the life of the man.

PAUL'S HOME

17. Paul had a certain pride in the place of his birth, as he showed by boasting on one occasion that he was a citizen of no mean city. He had a heart formed by nature to feel the warmest glow of patriotism. Yet it was not for Cilicia and Tarsus that this fire burned. He was an alien in the land of his birth. His father was one of those numerous Jews who was scattered in that age over the cities of the gentile world, engaged in trade and commerce. They had left the Holy Land, but they did not forget it. They never coalesced with the populations among whom they dwelt but, in dress, food, religion and many other particulars remained a peculiar people. As a rule, indeed, they were less rigid in their religious views and more tolerant of foreign customs than those Jews who remained in Palestine. But Paul's father was not one who had given way to laxity. He belonged to the straitest sect of his religion. It is probable that he had not left Palestine long before his son's birth, for Paul calls himself a Hebrew of the Hebrews—a name that seems to have belonged only to the Palestinian Jews and to those whose connection with Palestine had continued very close.

Of his mother we hear absolutely nothing, but everything seems to indicate that the home in which he was brought up was one of those out of which nearly all eminent religious teachers have sprung—a home of piety, of character, perhaps of somewhat stern principle, and of strong attachment to the peculiarities of a religious people. He was imbued with its spirit. Although he could not but receive innumerable and imperishable impressions from the city he was born in, the land and the city of his heart were Palestine and Jerusalem; and the heroes of his young imagination were not Curtius and Horatius, Hercules and Achilles, but Abraham and Joseph, Moses and David and Ezra. As he looked back on the past, it was not over the confused annals of Cilicia that he cast his eyes, but he gazed up the clear stream of Jewish history to its sources in Ur of the Chaldees, and when he thought of the future, the vision that came to him was the kingdom of the Messiah, enthroned in Jerusalem and ruling the nations with a rod of iron.

18. The feeling of belonging to a spiritual aristocracy, elevated above the majority of those among whom he lived, would be deepened in him by what he saw of the religion of the surrounding population. Tarsus was the center of a species of Baal worship of an imposing but unspeakably degrading character, and at certain seasons of the year it was the scene of festivals, which were frequented by the whole population of the neighboring regions, and were accompanied by orgies of a degree of moral abominableness happily beyond the reach even of our imaginations. Of course a boy could not see the depths of this mystery of iniquity, but he could see enough to make him turn from idolatry with the scorn peculiar to his nation, and to make him regard the little synagogue where his family worshiped the Holy One of Israel as far more glorious than the gorgeous temples of the heathen; and perhaps to these early experiences we may trace back in some degree those convictions of the depths to which human nature can fall and its need of an omnipotent redeeming force that afterward formed so fundamental a part of his theology and gave such a stimulus to his work.

TRADE

19. The time arrived for deciding what occupation the boy was to follow—a momentous crisis in every life—and in this case much was involved in the decision. Perhaps the most natural career for him would have been that of a merchant; because his father was engaged in trade, the busy city offered splendid prizes to mercantile ambition, and the boy's own energy would have guaranteed success. Besides, his father had an advantage to give him especially useful to a merchant: though a Jew, he was a Roman citizen, and this right would have given his son protection, into whatever part of the Roman world he might have had occasion to travel. How the father got this right we cannot tell; it could have been boughten, or won by distinguished service to the state, or acquired in several other ways; at all events his son was free-born. It was a valuable privilege, and one that was to prove of great use to Paul, though not in the way in which his father might have been expected to desire him to make use of it. But it was decided that he was not to be a merchant. The decision may have been due to his father's strong religious views, or his mother's pious ambition, or his own predilections; but it was resolved that he should go to college and become a rabbi—that is, a minister, a teacher, and a lawyer all in one. It was a wise decision in view of the boy's spirit and capabilities, and it turned out to be of infinite value for the future of mankind.

20. Although Paul had escaped the chances that seemed likely to pull him into a secular calling, yet, before going away to prepare for the sacred profession, he was to get some insight into business life; for it was a rule among the Jews that every boy, whatever might be the profession he was to follow, should learn a trade, as a resource in time of need. This was a rule with wisdom in it, for it gave employment to the young at an age when too much leisure is dangerous, and acquainted the wealthy and the learned in some degree with the feelings of those who have to earn their bread with the sweat of their brow. The trade that he was put to was the most common one in Tarsus—the making of tents from the goat's-hair cloth for which the district was celebrated. Little did he or his father think, when he began to handle the disagreeable material, of what importance this handicraft was to be to him in subsequent years. It became the means of his support during his missionary journeys, and, at a time when it was essential that the propagators of Christianity should be above suspicion of selfish motives, enabled him to maintain himself in a position of noble independence.

EDUCATION

21. A natural question to ask is whether, before leaving home to get his training as a rabbi, Paul attended the University of Tarsus. Did he drink at the wells of wisdom that flow from Mount Helicon before going to sit by those that spring from Mount Zion? From the fact that he makes two or three quotations from the Greek poets it has been inferred that he was acquainted with all the literature of Greece. But, on the other hand, it has been pointed out that his quotations are brief and commonplace, such as any man who spoke Greek would pick up and use occasionally; and the style and vocabulary of his Epistles are not those of the models of Greek literature, but of the Septuagint, the Greek version of the Hebrew

Scriptures, which was then in universal use among the Jews of the Dispersion. His father probably would have considered it sinful to allow his son to attend a heathen university. Yet it is not likely that he grew up in a great seat of learning without receiving some influence from the academic tone of the place. His speech at Athens shows that he was able, when he chose, to wield a style much more stately than that of his writings, and so keen a mind was not likely to remain in total ignorance of the great monuments of the language that he spoke.

22. There were other impressions, too, which the learned Tarsus probably made on him: its university was famous for those petty disputes and rivalries that sometimes ruffle the calm of academic retreats; and it is possible that the murmur of these, with which the air was often filled, may have given the first impulse to that scorn for the tricks of the rhetorician and the windy disputations of the sophist that form so marked a feature in some of his writings. The glances of young eyes are clear and sure, and even as a boy he may have perceived how small could be the souls of men and how mean their lives, when their mouths were filled with the finest phraseology.

23. The college for the education of Jewish rabbis was in Jerusalem, and there Paul was sent at about the age of thirteen. His arrival in the Holy City may have happened in the same year in which Jesus, at the age of twelve, first visited it, and the overpowering emotions of the boy from Nazareth at the first sight of the capital of His race may be taken as an index of the unrecorded experience of the boy from Tarsus. To every Jewish child of a religious disposition Jerusalem was the center of all things; the footsteps of prophets and kings echoed in the streets; memories sacred and sublime clung to its walls and buildings; and it shone in the glamor of illimitable hopes.

24. There is a chance that at this time the college of Jerusalem was presided over by one of the most noted teachers the Jews have ever possessed. This was Gamaliel, at whose feet Paul tells us he was brought up. He was called by his contemporaries the Beauty of the Law, and is still remembered among the Jews as the Great Rabbi. He was a man of lofty character and enlightened mind, a Pharisee strongly attached to the traditions of the fathers, yet not intolerant or hostile to Greek culture, as were some of the narrow-minded Pharisees. The influence of such a man on an open mind like Paul's must have been very great; and, although for a time the pupil became an intolerant zealot, yet the master's example may have had something to do with the conquest he finally won over prejudice.

25. The course of instruction that a rabbi had to undergo was long and unusual. It consisted entirely of the study of the Scriptures and the comments of the sages and masters on them. The words of Scripture and the sayings of the wise were committed to memory; discussions were carried on about disputed points; and by a rapid fire of questions, which the scholars were allowed to put as well as the masters, the wits of the students were sharpened and their views enlarged. The outstanding qualities of Paul's intellect, which were conspicuous in his subsequent life—his marvelous memory, the keenness of his logic, the superabundance of his ideas, and his original way of taking up every subject—first displayed themselves in this school, and excited, we may well believe, the warm interest of his teacher.

26. He himself learned much here that was of great importance to his subsequent career. Although he was to be especially the missionary to the Gentiles, he was also a great missionary to his own people. In every city he vis-

ited where there were Jews he made his first public appearance in the synagogue. There his training as a rabbi
secured him an opportunity of speaking, and his famil-
iarity with Jewish modes of thought and reasoning enabled him to address his audiences in the way best fitted to
secure their attention. His knowledge of the Scriptures
enabled him to adduce proofs from an authority that his
hearers acknowledged to be supreme.

Besides, he was destined to be the great theologian
of Christianity and the principal writer of the New Testament. Now the New grew out of the Old; the one is in all
its parts the prophecy and the other the fulfillment. But it
required a mind saturated not only with Christianity, but
with the Old Testament, to bring this out; and, at the age
when the memory is most retentive, Paul acquired such a
knowledge of the Old Testament that everything it contains was at his command: its phraseology became the
language of his thinking; he literally writes in quotations,
and he quotes from all parts with equal facility—from the
Law, the Prophets, and the Psalms. Thus was the warrior
equipped with the armor and the weapons of the Spirit
before he knew in what cause he was to use them.

HIS RELIGIOUS LIFE

27. Meantime what was his moral and religious
state? He was learning to be a religious teacher; was he
himself religious? Not all who are sent to college by their
parents to prepare for the sacred office are so, and in every
city of the world the path of youth is beset with temptations that may ruin life at its beginning. Some of the
greatest teachers of the church, such as St. Augustine,
have had to look back on half their life blotted and scarred
with vice or crime. No such fall defaced Paul's early years.
Whatever struggles with passion may have raged in his
own breast, his conduct was always pure. Jerusalem was

no very favorable place, in that age, for virtue. It was the Jerusalem against whose external sanctity, but internal depravity, our Lord a few years later hurled such withering invectives; it was the very seat of hypocrisy, where an able youth might easily have learned how to win the rewards of religion, while escaping its burdens. But Paul was preserved amidst these perils, and could later claim that he had lived in Jerusalem from the first in all good conscience.

28. He had brought with him from home the conviction, that forms the basis of a religious life, that the one prize that makes life worth living is the love and favor of God. This conviction grew into a passionate longing as he advanced in years, and he asked his teachers how the prize was to be won. Their answer was ready—by the keeping of the Law. It was a terrible answer; for the Law meant not only what we understand by the term, but also the ceremonial law of Moses and the thousand and one rules added to it by the Jewish teachers, the observance of which made life a purgatory to a tender conscience.

But Paul was not the man to shrink from difficulties. He had set his heart on winning God's favor, without which this life appeared to him a blank and eternity the blackness of darkness; and, if this was the way to the goal, he was willing to tread it. Not only, however, were his personal hopes involved in this, the hopes of his nation depended on it too; for it was the universal belief of his people that the Messiah would come only to a nation keeping the Law, and it was even said that, if one man kept it perfectly for a single day, his merit would bring to the earth the King for whom they were waiting. Paul's rabbinical training, then, culminated in the desire to win this prize of righteousness, and he left the halls of sacred learning with this as the purpose of his life. The lonely student's resolution was momentous for the world; for he was first to prove amidst secret agonies that this way of salvation was false, and then to teach his discovery to mankind.

AT JERUSALEM

29. We cannot tell in what year Paul's education at the college of Jerusalem was finished or where he went immediately afterward. The young rabbis, after completing their studies, scattered in the same way as our own theological students do, and began practical work in different parts of the Jewish world. He may have gone back to his native Cilicia and held office in some synagogue there. At all events, he was for some years at a distance from Jerusalem and Palestine; for these were the very years which saw the movement of John the Baptist and the ministry of Jesus, and it is certain that Paul could not have been in the vicinity without being involved in both of these movements either as a friend or as a foe.

30. But before long he returned to Jerusalem. It was as natural for the highest rabbinical talent to gravitate in those times to Jerusalem as it is for the highest literary and commercial talent to gravitate in our day to the metropolis. He arrived in the capital of Judaism soon after the death of Jesus; and we can easily imagine the representations of that event and of the career thereby terminated that he would receive from his Pharisaic friends.

We have no reason to suppose that as yet he had any doubts about his own religion. We gather from his writings that he had already passed through severe mental conflicts. Although the conviction still stood fast in his mind that the blessedness of life was attainable only in the favor of God, yet his efforts to reach this coveted position by the observance of the Law had not satisfied him. On the contrary, the more he strove to keep the law the more active became the motions of sin within him; his conscience was becoming more oppressed with the sense of guilt, and the peace of a soul at rest in God was a prize that eluded his grasp.

Still he did not question the teaching of the synagogue. To him as yet this was one with the history of the Old Testament, from which the figures of the saints and prophets looked down on him. They were a guarantee that the system they represented must be divine, and behind which he saw the God of Israel revealing Himself in the giving of the law. The reason why he had not attained to peace and fellowship with God was, he believed, because he had not struggled enough with the evil of his nature or honored enough the precepts of the Law. Was there no service by which he could make up for all deficiencies and win that grace at last in which the great of old had stood? This was the temper of mind in which he returned to Jerusalem, and learned with astonishment and indignation of the rise of a sect that believed that Jesus who had been crucified was the Messiah of the Jewish people.

STATE OF THE CHRISTIAN CHURCH

31. Christianity was as yet only two or three years old, and was growing very quietly in Jerusalem. Although those who had heard it preached at Pentecost had carried the news of it to their homes in many quarters, its public representatives had not yet left the city of its birth. At first the authorities had been inclined to persecute it, and checked its teachers when they appeared in public. But they had changed their minds and, acting under the advice of Gamaliel, resolved to neglect it, believing that it would die out, if left alone. The Christians, on the other hand, gave as little offense as possible; in the externals of religion they continued to be strict Jews and zealous of the

Law, attending the temple worship, observing the Jewish ceremonies, and respecting the ecclesiastical authorities.

It was a kind of truce, which allowed Christianity a little space for secret growth. In their upper rooms the brethren met to break bread and pray to their ascended Lord. It was the most beautiful spectacle. The new faith had alighted among them like an angel, and was shedding purity on their souls from its wings and breathing over their humble gatherings the spirit of peace. Their love to each other was unbounded; they were filled with the inspiring sense of discovery; and, as often as they met, their invisible Lord was in their midst. It was like heaven on earth. While Jerusalem around them was going on in its ordinary course of worldliness and ecclesiastical serenity, these few humble souls were making themselves happy with a secret that they knew to contain within it the blessedness of mankind and the future of the world.

32. But the truce could not last, and these scenes of peace were soon to be invaded with terror and bloodshed. Christianity could not keep such a truce, for there is in it a world-conquering force that impels it at all risks to propagate itself, and the fermentation of the new wine of gospel liberty was sure sooner or later to burst the forms of the Jewish law.

At length a man arose in the church in whom these aggressive tendencies embodied themselves. This was Stephen, one of the seven deacons who had been appointed to watch over the temporal affairs of the Christian society. He was a man full of the Holy Spirit and possessed of capabilities that the brevity of his career only permitted to suggest but not to develop themselves. He went from synagogue to synagogue, preaching the messiahship of Jesus and announcing the advent of freedom from the yoke of the Law. Champions of Jewish orthodoxy encountered him, but were not able to withstand his eloquence and holy zeal. Foiled in argument, they grasped at other weapons, stirring up the authorities and the populace to murderous fanaticism.

STEPHEN

33. One of the synagogues in which these disputations took place was that of the Cilicians, the countrymen of Paul. May he have been a rabbi in this synagogue and one of Stephen's opponents in argument? At all events, when the argument of logic was exchanged for that of violence, he was in the front. When the witnesses who cast the first stones at Stephen were stripping down for their work, they laid down their garments at his feet. There, on the margin of that wild scene, in the field of judicial murder, we see his figure, standing a little apart and sharply outlined against the mass of persecutors unknown to fame—the pile of many-colored robes at his feet, and his eyes bent on the holy martyr, who is kneeling in the article of death and praying: "Lord, lay not this sin to their charge."

THE PERSECUTOR

34. His zeal on this occasion brought Paul prominently under the notice of the authorities. It probably procured him a seat in the Sanhedrin, where we find him soon afterward casting his vote against the Christians. At all events, it led to his being entrusted with the work of utterly uprooting Christianity, which the authorities now resolved on. He accepted their proposal; for he believed it to be God's work. He saw more clearly than anyone else what was the drift of Christianity; and it seemed to him destined, if unchecked, to overturn all that he considered most sacred. The repeal of the Law was in his eyes the obliteration of the one way of salvation, and faith in a crucified Messiah blasphemy against the divinest hope of Israel. Besides, he had a deep personal interest in the task. Up to this point he had been striving to please God, but always felt his efforts to fall short; here was a chance to make up for all mistakes by one splendid act of service. This was the iron of agony in his soul that gave edge and energy to his zeal. In any case he was not a man to do things by halves; and he flung himself headlong into his task.

35. Terrible were the scenes that followed. He flew from synagogue to synagogue, and from house to house, dragging out men and women, who were cast into prison and punished. Some appear to have been put to death, and—darkest trait of all—others were compelled to blaspheme the name of the Savior. The church at Jerusalem was broken in pieces, and its members who escaped the rage of the persecutor were scattered over the neighboring provinces and countries.

36. It may seem too venturesome to call this the last stage of Paul's unconscious preparation for his apostolic career. But so it was. In entering on the career of a persecutor he was going on in the line of the creed in which he had been brought up; and this was its reduction to absurdity. Besides, through the gracious working of Him whose highest glory it is out of evil still to bring forth good, there sprang out of these sad doings in the mind of Paul an intensity of humility, a willingness to serve even the least of the brethren of those whom he had abused, and a zeal to redeem lost time by the parsimonious use of what was left, which became permanent spurs to action in his subsequent career.

3

HIS CONVERSION

SEVERITY OF THE PERSECUTION

37. It was the persecutor's hope to utterly exterminate Christianity. But little did he understand its genius. It thrives on persecution. Prosperity has often been fatal to it, persecution never. "They that were scattered abroad went everywhere preaching the word." Up to this time the church had been confined within the walls of Jerusalem; but now all over Judaea and Samaria, and in distant Phoenicia and Syria, the beacon of the gospel began in many a town and village to twinkle through the darkness, and twos and threes met together in upper rooms to impart to each other their joy in the Holy Spirit.

38. We can imagine with what rage the tidings of these outbreaks of the fanaticism that he had hoped to stamp out would fill the persecutor. But he was not the person to be hindered, and he resolved to hunt up the objects of his hatred even in their most obscure and distant hiding places. In one city after another he appeared, armed with the tools of the inquisitor, to carry his sanguinary purpose out. Having heard that Damascus, the capital of Syria, was one of the places where the fugitives had taken refuge, and that they were carrying on their propaganda among the numerous Jews of that city, he went to the high priest, who had jurisdiction over the Jews outside as well as inside Palestine, and got letters empowering him to seize and bind and bring to Jerusalem all of the new way of thinking whom he might find there.

KICKING AGAINST THE GOAD

39. As we see him start on this journey, which was to be so momentous, we naturally ask what was the state of his mind. His was a noble nature and a tender heart; but the work he was engaged in might be supposed to be congenial only to the most brutal of mankind. Had his mind, then, been visited with no compunctions? Apparently not. We are told that, as he was "marching" through distant cities in pursuit of his victims, he was exceedingly angry against them; and, as he set out to Damascus, he was still breathing out threatenings and slaughter. He was sheltered against doubt by his reverence for the objects that the heresy imperiled; and, if he had to outrage his natural feelings in the bloody work, was not his merit all the greater?

40. But on this journey doubt at last invaded his mind. It was a long journey of more than 160 miles; with the slow means of travel then available, it would take at least six days; and a considerable portion of it lay across a desert, where there was nothing to distract the mind from its own reflections. In this enforced leisure doubts arose. What else can be meant by the word with which the Lord saluted him: "It is hard for thee to kick against the goad!" The figure of speech is borrowed from a custom of Eastern countries: the ox driver wields a long pole, at the end of which is fixed a piece of sharpened iron, with which he urges the animal to go on or stand still or change its course; and, if it is obstinate, it kicks against the goad, injuring and infuriating itself with the wounds it receives. This is a vivid picture of a man wounded and tortured by compunctions of conscience. There was something in him rebelling against the course of inhumanity on which he was embarked and suggesting that he was fighting against God.

41. It is not difficult to conceive from where these doubts arose. Paul was a scholar of Gamaliel, the advocate of humanity and tolerance, who had counseled the Sanhedrin to leave the Christians alone. He was himself too young yet to have hardened his heart to all the disagreeables of such ghastly work. Highly strung as was his religious zeal, nature could not but speak out at last. But his compunctions were probably chiefly awakened by the character and behavior of the Christians. He had heard the noble defense of Stephen and had seen his face in the council chamber shining like that of an angel. He had seen him kneeling on the field of execution and praying for his murderers. Doubtless, in the course of the persecution he had witnessed many similar scenes. Did these people look like enemies of God? As he entered their homes to drag them to prison, he got glimpses of their social life. Could such spectacles of purity and love be products of the powers of darkness? Did not the serenity with which his victims went to meet their fate look like the very peace that he had long been sighing for in vain?

Their arguments, too, must have told on a mind like his. He had heard Stephen proving from the Scriptures that it was necessary for the Messiah to suffer; and the general tenor of the earliest Christian apologetic assures us that many of the accused at their trial must have appealed to passages like the fifty-third chapter of Isaiah, where a career is predicted for the Messiah startlingly like that of Jesus of Nazareth. He heard incidents of Christ's life from their lips that spoke of a person very different from the picture sketched for him by his pharisaic informants: and the sayings of their Master that the Christians quoted did not sound like the utterances of the fanatic he conceived Jesus to have been.

42. Such may have been some of the reflections that agitated the traveler as he moved onward, sunk in gloomy thought. But might not these be mere suggestions of temptation—the morbid fancies of a wearied mind, or the whispers of a wicked spirit attempting to draw him off from the service of heaven? The sight of Damascus, shining like a gem in the heart of the desert, restored him to himself. There, in the company of sympathetic rabbis and in the excitement of effort, he would dispel from his mind these fancies bred of solitude. So onward he pressed, and the sun of noonday, from which all but the most impatient travelers in the East take refuge in a long siesta, looked down on him still urging him onward toward the city gate.

THE VISION OF CHRIST

43. The news of Saul's coming reached Damascus before him; and the little flock of Christ was praying that, if it were possible, the progress of the wolf, who was on his way to spoil the fold, might be arrested. Nearer and nearer, however, he drew; he had reached the last stage of his journey; and at the sight of the place that contained his victims his appetite grew keener for the prey. But the Good Shepherd had heard the cries of the trembling flock and went forth to face the wolf on their behalf. Suddenly at midday, as Paul and his company were riding beneath the blaze of the Syrian sun, a light that dimmed even that fierce glare that shone around them, a shock vibrated through the atmosphere, and in a moment they found themselves prostrate on the ground. The rest was for Paul alone: a voice sounded in his ears, "Saul, Saul, why persecutest thou me?" and, as he looked up and asked the radiant figure that had spoken, "Who art thou, Lord?" the answer was, "I am Jesus, whom thou art persecuting."

44. The language in which he spoke of this event from that day on forbids us to think that it was a mere vision of Jesus he saw. He ranks it as the last of the appearances of the risen Savior to His disciples, and places it on the same level as the appearances to Peter, to James, to the eleven, and to the five hundred. It was, in fact, Christ Jesus in the vesture of His glorified humanity, who for once had left the spot, wherever it may be in the spaces of the universe, where now he sits on His mediatorial throne, in order to show Himself to this elect discipline; and the light that outshone the sun was no other than the glory in which His humanity is there enveloped. An incidental evidence of this was supplied in the words that were addressed to Paul. They were spoken in the Hebrew, or rather the Aramaic tongue—the same language in which Jesus had used to address the multitudes by the lake and converse with His disciples in the desert solitudes; and, as in the days of His flesh when He opened His mouth in parables, so now He clothed His rebuke in a striking metaphor: "It is hard for thee to kick against the goad."

EFFECT ON PAUL'S THOUGHT

45. It would be impossible to exaggerate what took place in the mind of Paul in this one instant. It is but a clumsy way we have of dividing time by the revolution of the clock into minutes and hours, days and years, as if each portion so measured were of the same size as another of equal length. This may suit well enough for the common ends of life, but there are finer measurements for which it is quite misleading. The real size of any space of time is to be measured by the amount it contains of the soul's experience; no one hour is exactly equal to another, and there are single hours that are larger than months. So measured, this one moment of Paul's life was perhaps larger than all his previous years. The glare of revelation was so intense that it might well have scorched the eye of reason or burned out life itself, as the external light dazzled the eyes of his body into blindness.

When his companions recovered themselves and turned to their leader, they discovered that he had lost his sight, and they had to take him by the hand and lead him into the city. What a change there was! Instead of the proud Pharisee riding through the streets with the pomp of an inquisitor, a stricken man, trembling, groping, clinging to the hand of his guide, arrives at the house of entertainment amidst the consternation of those who receive him and, going hastily to a room where he can ask them to leave him alone, sinks down there in the darkness.

46. But, though it was dark without, it was bright within. The blindness had been sent for the purpose of secluding him from outward distractions and enabling him to concentrate himself on the objects presented to the inner eye. For the same reason he neither ate nor drank for three days. He was too absorbed in the thoughts that crowded on him thick and fast.

47. In these three days, it may be said with confidence, he got at least a partial hold of all the truths he afterward proclaimed to the world; for his whole theology is nothing but the explication of his own conversion. First of all, his previous life fell in fragments at his feet. It had been of one piece, and wonderfully complete. It had appeared to him to be a consistent deducation from the highest revelation he knew and, in spite of its imperfections, to lie in the line of the will of God. But, instead of this, it had been rushing diametrically opposite the will and revelation of God, and had now been brought to a stop and been broken in pieces by the collision. That which had appeared to him the perfection of service and obedience had involved his soul in the guilt of blasphemy and innocent blood. Such had been the issue of seeking righteousness by the works of the law. At the moment when his righteousness seemed at last to be turning to the whiteness so long desired, it was caught in the blaze of this revelation and whirled away in shreds of shriveled blackness. It had been a mistake, then, from first to last. Righteousness was not to be obtained by the law, but only guilt and doom. This was the unmistakable conclusion, and it became the one pole of Paul's theology.

48. But, while his theory of life fell in pieces with a crash that might by itself have shaken his reason, in the same moment an opposite experience befell him. Jesus of Nazareth appeared to him, but not in wrath and vengeance as He might have been expected to appear to the deadly enemy of His cause. His first word might have been a demand for retribution, and His first might have been His last. Instead of this, His face had been full of divine kindness and His words full of consideration for His persecutor. In the very moment the divine strength cast him down on the ground he felt himself encompassed by the divine love. This was the prize he had all his lifetime been struggling for in vain, and now he grasped it in the very moment in which he discovered that his struggles had been fightings against God; he was lifted up from his fall in the arms of God's love; he was reconciled and accepted forever. As time went on, he was more and more assured of this. In Christ he found without effort of his own the peace and the moral strength he had striven for in vain. And this became the other pole of his theology—that righteousness and strength are found in Christ without man's effort by mere trust in God's grace and acceptance of His gift. There were a hundred other things involved in these two that required time to work out; but within these two poles the system of Paul's thinking ever afterward revolved.

EFFECT ON HIS FUTURE

49. The three dark days were not finished before he knew one thing more—that his life was to be devoted to the proclamation of these discoveries. In any case this must have been. Paul was a born propagandist and could not have become the possessor of such revolutionary truth without spreading it. Besides, he had a warm heart, that could be deeply moved with gratitude; and, when Jesus, whom he had blasphemed and tried to blot out of the memory of the world, treated him with such divine kindness, giving him back his forfeited life and placing him in the position that had always appeared to him the prize of life, he could not but put himself at His service with all his powers. He was an ardent patriot, the hope of the Messiah having long occupied for him the whole horizon of the future; and, when he knew that Jesus of Nazareth was the Messiah of his people and the Savior of the world, it followed as a matter of course that he must spend his life in making this known.

50. But this destiny was also clearly announced to him from the outside. Ananias, probably the leading man in the small Christian community at Damascus, was informed, in a vision, of the change that had happened to

Paul, and was sent to restore his sight and admit him into the Christian church by baptism.

Nothing could be more beautiful than the way in which this servant of God approached the man who had come to the city to take his life. As soon as he learned the state of the case, he forgave and forgot all the crimes of his enemy and sprang to clasp him in the arms of Christian love. Certain as may have been the assurance that in the inner world of the mind Paul had in those three days received of forgiveness, it must have been to him a most welcome reassurance when, on opening his eyes again on the external world, he was met with no contradiction of the visions he had been looking on, but the first object he saw was a human face bending over him with looks of forgiveness and perfect love. He learned from Ananias the future the Savior had appointed him: he had been apprehended by Christ in order to be a vessel to bear His name to Gentiles and kings and to the children of Israel. He accepted the mission with limitless devotion; and from that hour to the hour of his death he had but one ambition—to apprehend that for which he had been apprehended of Christ Jesus.

4

HIS GOSPEL

SOJOURN IN ARABIA

51. When a man has been suddenly converted, as
Paul was, he is generally driven by a strong impulse to
make known what has happened to him. Such testimony
is very impressive; for it is that of a soul that is receiving
its first glimpses of the realities of the unseen world, and
there is a vividness about the report it gives of them that
produces an irresistible sense of reality. Whether Paul
yielded at once to this impulse or not we cannot say with
certainty. The language of the Book of Acts, where it is
said that "straightway he preached Christ in the
synagogues," would lead us to suppose so. But we learn
from his own writings that there was another powerful
impulse influencing him at the same time; and it is un-
certain which of the two he obeyed first. This other impulse was the wish to retreat into solitude and think out
the meaning and issues of that which had befallen him.

We can imagine that this was a necessity. He had believed his former creed intensely and staked everything on it; to see it suddenly shattered in pieces must have shaken him severely. The new truth that had been flashed on him was so far-reaching and revolutionary that it could not all be taken in at once. Paul was a born thinker; it was not enough for him to experience anything; he needed to comprehend it and fit it into the structure of his convictions.

Immediately after his conversion, therefore, he went, he tells us, to Arabia. He does not say for what purpose he went; but, as there is no record of his preaching in that region and this statement occurs in the midst of a vehement defense of the originality of his gospel, we may conclude with considerable certainty that he went into retirement for the purpose of grasping in thought the details and the bearings of the revelation he had been put in possession of. In lonely contemplation he worked them out; and, when he returned to mankind, he was in possession of that view of Christianity that was peculiar to himself and formed the burden of his preaching during the subsequent years.

52. There is some doubt as to the precise place of his retirement, because Arabia is a word of vague and variable significance. But most probably it denotes the Arabia of the Wanderings, the principal feature of which was Mount Sinai. This was a spot hallowed by great memories and by the presence of other great men of revelation. Here Moses had seen the burning bush and communed with God on the top of the mountain. Here Elijah had roamed in his season of despair and drunk anew at the wells of inspiration. What place could be more appropriate for the meditations of this successor of these men of God? In the valleys where the manna fell and under the shadows of the peaks that had burned beneath the feet of Jehovah he pondered the problem of his life.

It is a great example. Originality in the preaching of the truth depends on the solitary intuition of it. Paul enjoyed the special inspiration of the Holy Spirit; but this did not render the concentrated activity of his own thinking unnecessary but only lent it peculiar intensity; and the clearness and certainty of his gospel were due to these months of sequestered thought. His retirement may have lasted a year or more; for between his conversion and his final departure from Damascus, to which he returned from Arabia, three years intervened; and one of them at least was spent in this way.

53. We have no detailed record of what the outlines of his gospel were until a period long following this; but, as these, when first they are traceable, are a mere form of the features of his conversion, and, as his mind was working so long and powerfully on the interpretation of that event at this period, there can be no doubt that the gospel sketched in the Epistles to the Romans and the Galatians was substantially the same as he preached from the beginning; and we are safe in inferring from these writings our account of his Arabian meditations.

FAILURE OF MAN'S RIGHTEOUSNESS

54. The starting point of Paul's thinking was still, as it had been from his childhood, the conviction, inherited from pious generations, that the true end and happiness of man lay in the enjoyment of the favor of God. This was to be attained through righteousness; only the righteous could God be at peace with and favor with His love. To attain righteousness must therefore be the chief end of man.

55. But man had failed to attain righteousness and had thereby come short of the favor of God, and exposed himself to the divine wrath. Paul proves this by taking a vast survey of the history of mankind in pre-Christian times in its two great sections—the Gentile and the Jewish.

56. The Gentiles failed. It might be supposed that they did not have the preliminary conditions for entering on the pursuit of righteousness because they did not enjoy the advantage of a special revelation. But Paul holds that even the heathen know enough of God to be aware of the obligation to follow after righteousness. There is a natural revelation of God in His works and in the human conscience sufficient to enlighten men as to this duty. But the heathen, instead of making use of this light, wantonly extinguished it. They were not willing to retain God in their knowledge and to bind themselves with the restraints that a pure knowledge of Him imposed. They corrupted the idea of God in order to feel at ease in an immoral life. The revenge of nature came on them in the darkening and confusion of their intellects. They fell into such insensate folly as to change the glorious and incorruptible nature of God into the images of men and beasts, birds and reptiles. This intellectual degeneracy was followed by still deeper moral degeneracy. God, when they forsook Him, let them go; and, when His restraining grace was removed, down they rushed into the depths of moral corruption. Lust and passion got the mastery of them, and their life became a mass of moral disease. In the end of the first chapter of Romans the features of their condition are sketched in colors that might be borrowed from the abode of devils, but were literally taken, as is too plainly proved by the pages even of gentile historians, from the condition of the cultured heathen nations at that time. This, then, was the history of one half of mankind: it had completely fallen from righteousness and exposed itself to the wrath of God, which is revealed from heaven against all unrighteousness of men.

57. The Jews were the other half of the world. Had they succeeded where the Gentiles had failed? They enjoyed, indeed, great advantages over the heathen; for they possessed the oracles of God, in which the divine nature was exhibited in a form that rendered it inaccessible to human perversion, and the divine law was written with equal plainness in the same form. But had they profited by these advantages? It is one thing to know the law and another thing to do it; but it is doing, not knowing, which is righteousness. Had they, then, fulfilled the will of God, which they knew?

Paul had lived in the same Jerusalem in which Jesus assailed the corruption and hypocrisy of scribes and Pharisees; he had looked closely at the lives of the representative men of his nation; and he does not hesitate to charge the Jews in mass with the very same sins as the Gentiles; no, he says that through them the name of God was blasphemed among the Gentiles. They boasted of their knowledge and were the bearers of the torch of truth, the fierce blaze of which exposed the sins of the heathen; but their religion was a bitter criticism of the conduct of others; they forgot to examine their own conduct by the same light; and, while they were repeating, Do not steal, Do not commit adultery, and a multitude of other commandments, they were indulging in these sins themselves. What good in these circumstances did their knowledge do them? It only condemned them more; for their sin was against light. While the heathen knew so little that their sins were comparatively innocent, the sins of the Jews were conscious and presumptuous. Their boasted superiority was therefore inferiority. They were more deeply condemned than the Gentiles they despised, and exposed to a heavier curse.

58. The truth is, Gentiles and Jews had both failed for the same reason. Trace these two streams of human life back to their sources and you come at last to a point where they are not two streams but one; and, before the division took place, something had happened that predetermined the failure of both. In Adam all fell, and from him all, both Gentiles and Jews, inherited a nature too weak for the arduous attainment of righteousness; human nature is carnal now, not spiritual, and therefore unequal to this supreme spiritual achievement.

The law could not alter this; it had no creative power to make the carnal spiritual. On the contrary, it aggravated the evil. It actually multiplied offenses, for its clear and full description of sins, which would have been an incomparable guide to a sound nature, turned into temptation for a morbid one. The very knowledge of sin tempts to its commission; the very command not to do anything is to a diseased nature a reason for doing it. This was the effect of the law: it multiplied and aggravated transgressions. And this was God's intention. Not that He was the author of sin; but, like a skillful physician, who at times has to use an instrument to bring a sore to a head before he heals it, He allowed the heathen to go their own way and gave the Jews the Law, that the sin of human nature might exhibit all its inherent qualities, before He intervened to heal it. The healing, however, was His real purpose all the time: He concluded all were under sin, that He might have mercy on all.

THE RIGHTEOUSNESS OF GOD

59. Man's extremity was God's opportunity; not, indeed, in the sense that, one way of salvation having failed, God devised another. The Law had never, in His intention, been a way of salvation. But the moment when this demonstration was complete was the signal for God to produce His method, which He had kept locked in His counsel through the generations of human probation. It had never been His intention to permit man to fail of his true end. He just allowed time to prove that fallen man could never reach righteousness by his own efforts; and, when the righteousness of man had been demonstrated to be a failure, He brought forth His secret—the righteousness of God.

This was Christianity; this was the sum and issue of the mission of Christ—the conferring on man, as a free gift, of that which is indispensable to his blessedness, but which he had failed himself to attain. It is a divine act; it is grace; and man obtains it by acknowledging that he has failed himself to attain it and by accepting it from God; it is received by faith only. It is "the righteousness of God, by the faith of Jesus Christ, unto all and upon all them that believe."

60. Those who receive it in this manner enter at once into that position of peace and favor with God in which human happiness consists and which was the goal aimed at by Paul when he was striving for righteousness by the Law. "Being justified by faith, we have peace with God through our Lord Jesus Christ, by whom also we have access by faith into this grace wherein we stand, and rejoice in hope of the glory of God." It is a sunny life of joy, peace, and hope that those lead who have come to know this gospel. There may be trials in it; but, when a man's life reposes in the attainment of its true end, trials are light and all things work together for good.

61. This righteousness of God is for all the children of men—not for the Jews only, but for the Gentiles also. The demonstration of man's inability to attain righteousness was made, in accordance with the divine purpose, in both sections of the human race; and its completion was the signal for the exhibition of God's grace to both alike. The work of Christ was not for the children of Abraham, but for the children of Adam. "As in Adam all died, so in Christ shall all be made alive." The Gentiles did not need to undergo circumcision and to keep the Law in order to obtain salvation; for the Law was no part of salvation; it belonged entirely to the preliminary demonstration of man's failure; and, when it had accomplished this service, it was ready to vanish. The only human condition of obtaining God's righteousness is faith; and this is as easy for Gentile as Jew.

This was an inference from Paul's own experience. It was not as a Jew, but as a man, that he had been dealt with in his conversion. No Gentile could have been less entitled to obtain salvation by merit than he had been. So far from the Law raising him a single step toward salvation, it had removed him to a greater distance from God than any Gentile, and cast him into a deeper condemnation. How, then, could it profit the Gentiles to be placed in this position? In obtaining the righteousness in which he was now rejoicing he had done nothing that was not competent to any human being.

62. It was this universal love of God revealed in the gospel that inspired Paul with unbounded admiration for Christianity. His sympathies had been cabined, cribbed, confined in a narrow conception of God; the new faith uncaged his heart and sent it forth into the free and sunny air. God became a new God to him. He calls his discovery the mystery that had been hidden from ages and generations, but had been revealed to him and his fellow apostles. It seemed to him to be the secret of the ages and to be destined to usher in a new era, far better than any the world had ever seen. What kings and prophets had not known had been revealed to him. It had burst on him like the dawn of a new creation. God was now offering to every man the supreme happiness of life—that righteousness that had been the vain endeavor of the past ages.

63. This secret of the new era had not, indeed, been entirely unanticipated in the past. It had been "witnessed by the law and the prophets." The Law could bear witness to it only negatively by demonstrating its necessity. But the prophets anticipated it more positively. David, for example, described "the blessedness of the man unto whom God imputed righteousness without works." Still more clearly had Abraham anticipated it. He was a justified man; and it was by faith, not by works, that He was justified—"he believed God, and it was imputed unto him for righteousness." The Law had nothing to do with his justification, for it was not in existence for four centuries afterward. Nor had circumcision anything to do with it, for he was justified before this rite was instituted. In short, it was as a man, not as a Jew, that he was dealt with by God, and God might deal with any human being in the same way. It had once made the thorny road of legal righteousness sacred to Paul to think that Abraham and the prophets had trodden it before him; but now he knew that their life of religious joy and psalms of holy calm were inspired by quite different experiences, which were now diffusing the peace of heaven through his heart also. But only the first streaks of dawn had been detected by them; the perfect day had broken in his own time.

THE OLD ADAM AND THE NEW

64. Paul's discovery of this way of salvation was an actual experience; he simply knew that Christ, in the moment when He met him, had placed him in that position of peace and favor with God that he had long sighed for in vain, and, as time went on, he felt more and more that in this position he was enjoying the true blessedness of life. His mission from now was to herald this discovery in its simple and concrete reality under the name of the righteousness of God. But a mind like his could not help inquiring how it was that the possession of Christ did so much for him. In the Arabian wilderness he pondered over this question, and the gospel he subsequently preached contained a luminous answer to it.

65. From Adam his children derive a sad double heritage—a debt of guilt which they cannot reduce but are constantly increasing, and a carnal nature which is incapable of righteousness. These are the two features of the religious condition of fallen man, and they are the double source of all his woes.

But Christ is a new Adam, a new head of humanity, and those who are connected with Him by faith become heirs of a double heritage of a precisely opposite kind. On the one hand, just as through our birth in the first Adam's line we become inevitably entangled in guilt, like a child born into a family which is drowned in debt, so through our birth in the line of the second Adam we get involved in a boundless heritage of merit, which Christ, as the Head of His family, makes the common property of its members. This extinguishes the debt of our guilt and makes us rich in Christ's righteousness. "As by one man's disobedience many were made sinners, so by the obedience of one shall many be made righteous." On the other hand, just as Adam transmitted to his posterity a carnal nature, alien to God and unfit for righteousness, so the new Adam imparts to the race of which He is the Head a spiritual nature, akin to God and delighting in righteousness.

The nature of man, according to Paul, normally consists of three sections—body, soul, and spirit. In his original constitution these occupied definite relations of superiority and subordination to one another, the spirit being supreme, the body least important, and the soul occupying the middle position. But the Fall disarranged this order, and all sin consists in the usurpation by the body or the soul of the place of the spirit. In fallen man these two inferior sections of human nature, which together form what Paul calls the "flesh," or that side of human nature that looks toward the world and time, have taken possession of the throne and completely rule the life, while the spirit, the side of man that looks toward God and eternity, has been dethroned and reduced to a condition of inefficiency and death. Christ restores the lost predominance of the spirit of man by taking possession of it by His own Spirit. His Spirit dwells in the human spirit, vivifying it and sustaining it in such growing strength that it becomes more and more the sovereign part of the human constitution. The man ceases to be carnal and becomes spiritual; he is led by the Spirit of God and becomes more and more harmonious with all that is holy and divine.

The flesh does not, indeed, easily submit to the loss of supremacy. It clogs and obstructs the spirit and fights to regain possession of the throne. Paul has described this struggle in sentences of stark vividness, in which all generations of Christians have recognized the features of their deepest experience. But the issue of the struggle is not doubtful. Sin shall not again have dominion over those in whom Christ's Spirit dwells, or dislodge them from their standing in the favor of God. "Neither death, nor life, nor angels, nor principalities nor powers, nor things present, nor things to come, nor height, nor depth, nor any other creature, shall be able to separate us from the love of God, which is in Christ Jesus our Lord."

THE PAULINE GOSPEL

66. Such are the bare outlines of the gospel that Paul brought back with him from the Arabian solitudes and afterward preached with unwearied enthusiasm. It could not but be mixed up in his mind and in his writings with the peculiarities of his own experience as a Jew, and these make it difficult for us to grasp his system in some of its details. The belief in which he was brought up, that no man could be saved without becoming a Jew, and the notions about the Law from which he had to cut himself free, lie distant from our modern sympathies; yet his theology could not shape itself in his mind except in contrast to these misconceptions. This became subsequently still more inevitable when his own old errors met him as the watchwords of a party within the Christian church itself, against which he had to wage a long and relentless war. Though this conflict forced his views into the clearest expression, it encumbered them with references to feelings and beliefs that are now dead to the interest of mankind. But, in spite of these drawbacks, the gospel of Paul remains a possession of incalculable value to the human race. Its searching investigation of the failure and the wants of human nature, its wonderful unfolding of the wisdom of God in the education of the pre-Christian world, and its exhibition of the depth and universality of the divine love are among the profoundest elements of revelation.

67. But it is in its conception of Christ that Paul's gospel wears its imperishable crown. The evangelists sketched in a hundred traits of simple and affecting beauty the fashion of the earthly life of the man Christ Jesus, and in these the model of human conduct will always have to be sought; but to Paul was reserved the task of making known, in its heights and depths, the work which the Son of God accomplished as the Savior of the race. He scarcely ever refers to the incidents of Christ's earthly life, although here and there he betrays that he knew them well. To him Christ was ever the glorious Being, shining with the splendor of heaven, who appeared to him on the way to Damascus, and the Savior

who caught him up into the heavenly peace and joy of a new life. When the church of Christ thinks of her Head as the deliverer of the soul from sin and death, as a spiritualizing presence ever with her and at work in every believer, and as the Lord over all things who will come again without sin unto salvation, it is in forms of thought given her by the Holy Spirit through the instrumentality of this apostle.

5

THE WORK
AWAITING THE WORKER

YEARS OF INACTIVITY

68. Paul was now in possession of his gospel and was aware that it was to be the mission of his life to preach it to the Gentiles; but he still had to wait a long time before his unique career began. We hear scarcely anything of him for seven or eight years; and yet we can only guess what may have been the reasons of Providence for imposing on His servant so long a time of waiting.

69. There may have been personal reasons for it connected with Paul's own spiritual history; because waiting is a common instrument of providential discipline for those to whom exceptional work has been appointed. A public reason may have been that he was too obnoxious to the Jewish authorities to be tolerated yet in those scenes where Christian activity commanded any notice. He had attempted to preach in Damascus, where his conversion had taken place, but was immediately forced to flee from the fury of the Jews; and, going from there to Jerusalem and beginning to testify as a Christian, he found the place in two or three weeks too hot to hold him. No wonder; how could the Jews be expected to allow the man who had so lately been the chief champion of their religion to preach the faith they had employed him to destroy? When he fled from Jerusalem, he turned his steps to his native Tarsus, where for years he remained in obscurity. No doubt he testified for Christ there to his own family, and there are some indications that he carried on evangelistic operations in his native province of Cilicia: but, if he did, his work may be said to have been that of a man in hiding, for it was not in the central or even in a visible stream of the new religious movement.

70. These are but conjectural reasons for the obscurity of those years. But there was one undoubted reason for the delay of Paul's career of the greatest possible importance. In this interval took place that revolution—one of the most momentous in the history of mankind—by which the Gentiles were admitted to equal privileges with the Jews in the church of Christ. This change proceeded from the original circle of apostles, in Jerusalem, and Peter, the chief of the apostles, was the instrument of it. By the vision of the sheet of clean and unclean beasts, which he saw at Joppa, he was prepared for the part he was to play in this transaction, and he admitted the gentile Cornelius, of Caesarea, and his family to the church by baptism without circumcision. This was an innovation involving boundless consequences. It was a necessary preliminary to Paul's mission work, and subsequent events were to show how wise was the divine arrangement that the first gentile entrants into the church should be admitted by the hands of Peter rather than by those of Paul.

71. As soon as this event had taken place, the arena was clear for Paul's career, and a door was immediately opened for his entrance upon it. Almost simultaneously with the baptism of the gentile family at Caesarea a great revival broke out among the Gentiles of the city of Antioch, the capital of Syria. The movement had been begun by fugitives driven by persecution from Jerusalem, and it was carried on with the sanction of the apostles, who sent Barnabas, one of their trusted bishops, from Jerusalem to superintend it.

This man knew Paul. When Paul first came to Jerusalem after his conversion and sought to join himself to the Christians there, they were all afraid of him, suspecting the teeth and claws of the wolf beneath the fleece of the sheep. But Barnabas rose above these fears and suspicions and, having taken the new convert and having heard his story, believed in him and persuaded the rest to receive him. The intercourse thus begun only lasted a week or two at that time, as Paul had to leave Jerusalem; but Barnabas had received a profound impression of his personality and did not forget him. When he was sent down to superintend the revival at Antioch, he soon found himself embarrassed with its magnitude and in need of assistance; and the idea occurred to him that Paul was the man he wanted. Tarsus was not far off, and he went there to seek him. Paul accepted his invitation and returned with him to Antioch.

72. The hour he had been waiting for had struck, and he threw himself into the work of evangelizing the Gentiles with the enthusiasm of a great nature that found itself at last in its proper sphere. The movement at once responded to the pressure of such a hand; the disciples became so numerous and prominent that the heathen gave them a new name—that name of "Christians," which has ever since continued to be the badge of faith in

Christ—and Antioch, a city of half a million inhabitants, instead of Jerusalem, became the headquarters of Christianity. Soon a large church was formed, and one of the manifestations of the zeal with which it was pervaded was a proposal, which gradually shaped itself into an enthusiastic resolution, to send forth a mission to the heathen. As a matter of course, Paul was designated for this service.

THE KNOWN WORLD OF THAT PERIOD

73. As we see him brought at length face to face with the task of his life, let us pause to take a brief survey of the world he was setting out to conquer. Nothing less was what he aimed at. In Paul's time the known world was so small a place that it did not seem impossible even for a single man to make a spiritual conquest of it; and it had been wonderfully prepared for the new force that was about to assail it.

74. It consisted of a narrow disc of land surrounding the Mediterranean Sea. That sea deserved at that time the name it bears, for the world's center of gravity, which has since shifted to other latitudes, lay in it. The interest of human life was concentrated in the southern countries of Europe, the portion of western Asia and the strip of northern Africa that form its shores. In this little world there were three cities that divided between them the interest of those ages. These were Rome, Athens, and Jerusalem, the capitals of the three races—the Romans, the Greeks, and the Jews—which in every sense ruled that old world. It was not that each of them had mastered a third part of the circle of civilization, but each of them had in turn diffused itself over the whole of it, and either still held its grip or at least had left imperishable traces of its presence.

75. The Geeks were the first to take possession of the world. They were the people of cleverness and genius, the perfect masters of commerce, literature, and art. In very early ages they displayed the instinct for colonization and sent their sons to find new abodes on the east and the west, far from their native home. In time there arose among them one who concentrated in himself the strongest tendencies of the race and by force of arms extended the dominion of Greece to the borders of India. The vast empire of Alexander the Great divided into pieces at his death; but a deposit of Greek life and influence remained in all the countries over which the deluge of his conquering armies had swept. Greek cities, such as Antioch in Syria and Alexandria in Egypt, flourished all over the East; Greek merchants abounded in every center of trade; Greek teachers taught the literature of their country in many lands; and—what was most important of all—the Greek language became the general vehicle for the communication of the more serious thought between nation and nation. Even the Jews in New Testament times read their own Scriptures in a Greek version, the original Hebrew having become a dead language. Perhaps the Greek is the most perfect tongue the world has known, and there was a special providence in its universal diffusion before Christianity needed a medium of international communication. The New Testament was written in Greek, and, wherever the apostles of Christianity traveled, they were able to make themselves understood in this language.

76. The Romans were the next to gain possession of the world. Originally a small clan in the neighborhood of the city from which they derived their name, they gradually extended and strengthened themselves and acquired such skill in the arts of war and government that they became irresistible conquerors and marched forth in every direction to make themselves masters of the globe. They subdued Greece itself and, flowing eastward, seized the countries that Alexander and his successors had ruled. The whole known world became theirs from the Straits of Gibralter to the far East. They did not possess the genius or geniality of the Greeks; their qualities were strength and justice; and their arts were not those of the poet and the thinker, but those of the soldier and the judge. They broke down the divisions between the tribes of men and compelled them to be friendly toward each other, because they were all equally prostrate beneath one iron rule. They pierced the countries with roads, which connected them with Rome, and were such solid triumphs of engineering skill that some of them remain to this day. Along with these highways the message of the gospel ran. Thus the Romans also proved to be pioneers for Christianity, for their authority in so many countries afforded its first publishers facility of movement and protection from the arbitrary justice of local tribunals.

77. Meanwhile, the third nation of antiquity had also completed its conquest of the world, although not by force of arms as the Greeks and Romans had done. For centuries they had dreamed of the coming of a warlike hero, whose prowess should outshine that of the most celebrated gentile conquerors. But he never came: and their occupation of the centers of civilization had to take place in a more silent way.

There is no change in the habits of any nation more striking than that which passed over the Jewish race in the interval of four centuries between Malachi and Matthew of which we have no record in the sacred Scriptures. In the Old Testament we see the Jews confined within the narrow limits of Palestine, engaged mainly in agricultural pursuits and jealously guarding themselves from intermingling with foreign nations. In the New

Testament we find them still clinging with a desperate tenacity to Jerusalem and to the idea of their own separateness. But their habits and life style have been completely changed: they have given up agriculture and have been engaged with extraordinary eagerness and success in commerce; and with this object in view they diffused themselves everywhere—over Africa, Asia, Europe—there is not a city of any importance where they are not to be found. By what steps this extraordinary change came about it would be hard to tell and difficult to trace. But it had taken place; and this turned out to be a circumstance of extreme importance for the early history of Christianity.

Wherever the Jews were settled, they had their synagogues, their sacred Scriptures, their uncompromising belief in the one true God. Not only so: their synagogues everywhere attracted proselytes from the surrounding gentile populations. The heathen religions were at that period in a state of utter collapse. The smaller nations had lost faith in their deities because they had not been able to defend them from the victorious Greeks and Romans. But the conquerors had for other reasons equally lost faith in their own gods. It was an age of skepticism, religious decay, and moral corruption. But there are always natures that must possess a faith in which they can trust. These were in search of a religion, and many of them found refuge from the coarse and incredible myths of the gods of polytheism in the purity and monotheism of the Jewish creed. The fundamental ideas of this creed are also the foundations of the Christian fatih. Wherever the messengers of Christianity traveled, they met with people with whom they had many religious conceptions in common. Their first sermons were delivered in synagogues, their first converts were Jews and proselytes. The synagogue was the bridge by which Christianity crossed over to the heathen.

78. Such, then, was the world Paul was setting out to conquer. It was a world everywhere pervaded with these three influences. But there were two other elements of population that must be kept in mind, as both of them supplied numerous converts to the early preachers: they were the original inhabitants of the various countries; and there were the slaves, who were either captives taken in war or their descendants, and were liable to be shifted from place to place, being sold according to the necessities or caprices of their masters. A religion, the chief boast of which was to preach glad tidings to the poor, could not neglect these downtrodden classes, and, although the conflict of Christianity with the forces of time that had possession of the fate of the world naturally attracts attention, it must not be forgotten that its best triumph has always consisted in the sweetening and brightening of the lot of the humble.

6

HIS MISSIONARY TRAVELS

THE FIRST JOURNEY

79. From the beginning it had been the custom of the preachers of Christianity not to go alone on their expeditions, but to go two by two. Paul improved on this practice by going generally with two companions, one of them being a younger man, who perhaps took charge of the traveling arrangements. On his first journey his comrades were Barnabas and John Mark, the nephew of Barnabas.

80. We have already seen that Barnabas may be called the discoverer of Paul; and, when they set out on this journey together, he was probably in a position to act as Paul's patron, for he was well thought of in the Christian community. Converted apparently on the day of Pentecost, he had played a leading part in the subsequent events. He was a man of high social position, a proprietor of land on the island of Cyprus; and he sacrificed all to the new movement into which he had been drawn. In the outburst of enthusiasm that led the first Christians to share their property with one another, he sold his estate and laid the money at the apostles' feet. He was constantly employed thereafter in the work of preaching, and he had such a remarkable gift of eloquence that he was called the Son of Exhortation. An incident that occurred at a later stage of this journey gives us a glimpse of the appearance of the two men. When the inhabitants of Lystra mistook them for gods, they called Barnabas Jupiter and Paul Mercury. Now, in ancient art Jupiter was always represented as a tall, majestic, and kind figure, while Mercury was the small, swift messenger of the father of gods and men. It probably appeared therefore that the large, gracious, paternal Barnabas was the head and director of the expedition, while Paul, little and eager, was the subordinate. The direction in which they set out was also the one that Barnabas might naturally have been expected to choose. They went first to Cyprus, the island where his property had been and many of his friends still were. It lay eighty miles to the southwest of Seleucia, the seaport of Antioch, and they might reach it on the very day they left their headquarters.

81. At Cyprus his name was changed. Although Barnabas appeared to be the leader, the good man probably knew already that the humble words of the Baptist might be used by himself with reference to his companion, "He must increase, but I must decrease." At any event, as soon as their work began in earnest, this was shown to be the relationship between them. After going through the length of the island, from east to west, evangelizing, they arrived at Paphos, its chief town, and there the problems they had come out to face met them in the most concentrated form.

Paphos was the seat of the worship of Venus, the goddess of love, who was said to have been born of the foam of the sea at this very spot; and her worship was carried on with the wildest licentiousness. It was a picture in miniature of Greece sunk in moral decay. Paphos was also the seat of the Roman government, and in the proconsular chair sat a man, Sergius Paulus, whose noble character but utter lack of certain faith formed a companion picture of the inability of Rome at that time to meet the deepest needs of her best sons. In the proconsular court, playing on the inquirer's credulity, a Jewish sorcerer and quack, named Elymas, was flourishing, whose arts were a picture of the lowest depths to which the Jewish character could sink. The whole scene was a kind of miniature of the world the evils of which the missionaries had set out to cure.

In the presence of these exigencies Paul unfolded for the first time the mighty powers that lay in him. An access of the spirit seizing him and enabling him to overcome all obstacles, he covered the Jewish magician with disgrace, converted the Roman governor, and founded in the town a Christian church in opposition to the Greek shrine. From that hour Barnabas dropped into second place and Paul took his natural position as the head of the mission. We no longer read, as before, of "Barnabas and Saul," but always of "Paul and Barnabas." The subordinate had become the leader; and, as if to mark that he had become a new man and taken a new place, he was no longer called by the Jewish name of Saul, which up to this point he had borne, but by the name of Paul, which has ever since been his designation among Christians.

82. The next move was as obviously the choice of the new leader as the first one had been due to Barnabas and that was that they would to to the mainland of Asia. They sailed across the sea to Perga, a town near the middle of the southern coast of Asia Minor, then straight up a hundred miles into the mainland, and from there eastward to a point almost straight north of Tarsus. This route carried them in a kind of half circuit through the districts of Pamphylia, Pisidia, and Lycaonia, which border, to the west and north, on Cilicia, Paul's native province. So if he had already evangelized Cilicia, he was now merely extending his labors to the nearest surrounding regions.

83. At Perga, the starting point of this second half of the journey, a misfortune befell the expedition: John Mark deserted his companions and sailed for home. It may be that the new position assumed by Paul had offended him, though his generous uncle felt no such grudge at that which was the decree of nature and of God. But it is more likely that the cause of his withdrawal was dismay at the dangers on which they were about to enter. These were such as might well strike terror even into resolute hearts. Behind Perga rose the snow-clad peaks of the Taurus Mountains, which had to be penetrated through narrow passes, where crazy bridges spanned the rushing torrents, and the castles of robbers, who watched for passing travelers to pounce upon, were hidden in postions so inaccessible that even the Roman arms had not been able to exterminate them. When these preliminary dangers were surmounted, the prospect beyond was anything but inviting: the country to the north of the Taurus was a vast tableland, more elevated than the summits of the highest mountains in this country, and scattered with solitary lakes, irregular mountain masses and tracts of desert, where the population was rude and spoke an almost endless variety of dialects. These things terrified Mark, and he drew back. But his companions took their lives in their hands and went forward. To them it was enough that there were multitudes of perishing souls there, needing the salvation of which they were the heralds; and Paul knew that there were scattered handfuls of his own people in these remote regions of the heathen.

84. Can we conceive what their procedure was like in the towns they visited? It is difficult to picture it to ourselves. As we try to see them with the mind's eye entering any place, we naturally think of them as the most important personages in it; to us their entry is as august as if they had been carried on a car of victory. In reality it was very different, however. They entered a town as quietly and as unnoticed as any two strangers who may enter one of our towns any morning. Their first concern was to get a lodging; and then they had to seek for employment, for they worked at their trade wherever they went. Nothing could be more commonplace. Who could dream that this travel-stained man, going from one tentmaker's door to another, seeking for work, was carrying the future of the world beneath his robe!

When the Sabbath came around, they would cease from toil, like the other Jews in the place, and move to the synagogue. They joined in the psalms and prayers with the other worshipers and listened to the reading of the Scriptures. After this the presiding elder might ask if anyone present had a word of exhortation to deliver. This was Paul's opportunity. He would rise and, with outstretched hand, begin to speak. At once the audience recognized the accents of the cultivated rabbi: and the unfamiliar voice won their attention. Taking up the passages that had been read, he would soon move forward on the stream of Jewish history, until he led up to the astounding announcement that the Messiah hoped for by their fathers and promised by their prophets had come; and he had been sent among them as His apostle. Then would follow the story of Jesus; it was true, He had been rejected by the authorities of Jerusalem and crucified, but this could be shown to have taken place in accordance with prophecy; and His resurrection from the dead was an infallible proof that He had been sent of God: now He was exalted a Prince and Savior to give repentance to Israel and the remission of sins.

We can easily imagine the sensation produced by such a sermon from such a preacher and the buzz of conversation that would arise among the congregation after the dismissal of the synagogue. During the week it would become the talk of the town: and Paul was willing to converse at his work or in the leisure of the evening with any who might desire further information. The next Sabbath the synagogue would be crowded, not with Jews only, but Gentiles also, who were curious to see the strangers; and Paul would then unfold the secret that salvation by Jesus Christ was as free to Gentiles as to Jews. This was generally the signal for the Jews to contradict and blaspheme; and, turning his back on them, Paul would address himself to the Gentiles. But meantime the fanaticism of the Jews was roused, who either stirred up the mob or secured the interest of the authorities against the strangers; and in a storm of popular tumult or by the breath of authority the messengers of the gospel were forced out of the town. This was what happened at Antioch in Pisidia, their first stopping place in the interior of Asia Minor; and it was repeated in a hundred instances in Paul's subsequent life.

85. Sometimes they did not get off so easily. At Lystra, for example, they found themselves in a city of rude heathens, who were at first so charmed with Paul's winning words and were so impressed with the appearance of the preachers that they took them for gods and were on the point of offering sacrifice to them. This filled the missionaries with horror, and they rejected the intentions of the crowd with unceremonious haste. A sudden revolution in the popular sentiment followed and Paul was stoned and cast out of the city apparently dead.

86. Such were the scenes of excitement and peril through which they had to pass in this remote region. But their enthusiasm never flagged; they never thought of turning back, but, when they were driven out of one city, they moved forward to another. And, as total as their discomfitures sometimes appeared, they left no city without leaving behind them a little band of converts— perhaps a few Jews, a few more proselytes, and a number of Gentiles. The gospel found those for whom it was intended—penitents burdened with sin, souls dissatisfied with the world and their ancestral religion, hearts yearning for divine sympathy and love; "as many as were ordained to eternal life believed"; and these formed in every city the nucleus of a Christian church. Even at Lystra, where the defeat seemed so utter, a little group of faithful hearts gathered around the mangled body of the apostle outside the city gates; Eunice and Lois were there with tender womanly service; and young Timothy, as he looked down on the pale and bleeding face, felt his heart forever knit to the hero who had courage to suffer to the death for his faith.

87. In the intense love of such hearts Paul received compensation for suffering and injustice. If, as some suppose, the people of this region formed part of the Galatian churches, we see from his epistle to them the kind of love they gave him. They received him, he says, as an angel of God, no, as Jesus Christ Himself; they were ready to have plucked out their eyes and given them to him. They were people of rude kindness and headlong impulses; their native religion was one of excitement and demonstrative-ness, and they carried these characteristics into the new faith they had adopted. They were filled with joy and the Holy Spirit, and the revival spread on every hand with great rapidity, until the word, sounding out from the little Christian communities, was heard all along the slopes of Taurus and down the glens of the Cestrus and Halys.

Paul's warm heart could not help but enjoy such an outburst of affection. He responded to it by giving in return his own deep love. The towns mentioned in their itinerary are the Pisidian Antioch, Iconium, Lystra, and Derbe; but, when at the last of them he had finished his course and the way lay open to him to descend by the Cilician Gates to Tarsus and from there return to Antioch, he preferred to return by the way he had come. In spite of the most imminent danger he revisited all these places, to see his dear converts again, and to cheer them in face of persecution; and he ordained elders in every city to watch over the churches in his absence.

88. In time the missionaries descended again from these uplands to the southern coast and sailed back to Antioch, from where they had set out. Worn with toil and suffering, but flushed with the joy of success, they ap-peared among those who had sent them forth and had doubtless been following them with their prayers; and, like discoverers returned from the finding of a new coun-try, they related the miracles of grace they had witnessed in the strange world of the heathen.

THE SECOND JOURNEY

89. In his first journey Paul may be said to have been only trying his wings; for his course, adventurous though it was, only swept in a limited circle around his native province. In his second journey he performed a far more distant and perilous flight. Indeed, this journey was not only the greatest he achieved but perhaps the most momentous recorded in the annals of the human race. In its issues it far outrivaled the expedition of Alexander the Great, when he carried the arms and civilization of Greece into the heart of Asia, or that of Caesar, when he landed on the shores of Britain, or even the voyage of Columbus, when he discovered a new world. Yet, when he set out on it, he had no idea of the magnitude that it was to assume or even the direction it was to take. After enjoying a short rest at the close of the first journey, he said to his fellow missionary, "Let us go again and visit our brethren in every city where we have preached the word of the Lord and see how they do." It was the parental longing to see his spiritual children that was drawing him; but God had far more extensive designs, which opened up before him as he went forward.

90. Unfortunately, the beginning of this journey was marred by a dispute between the two friends who meant to travel together. The occasion of their difference was the offer of John Mark to accompany them. No doubt when this young man saw Paul and Barnabas returning safe and sound from the undertaking he had deserted, he recognized what a mistake he had made; and he now wished to correct his error by rejoining them. Barnabas naturally wished to take his nephew, but Paul absolutely refused. The one missionary, a man of easy kindliness, urged the duty of forgiveness and the effect that a rebuff might have on a beginner; while the other, full of zeal for God, represented the danger of making so sacred a work in any way dependent on one who could not be relied upon, for "confidence in an unfaithful man in time of trouble is like a broken tooth or a foot out of joint."

We cannot now tell which of them was in the right or if both were partly wrong. Both of them, at all events, suffered for it: Paul had to part in anger from the man to whom he probably owed more than to any other human being; and Barnabas was separated from the grandest spirit of the age.

91. They never met again. This was not due, however, to an unchristian continuation of the quarrel, for the heat of passion soon cooled down and the old love returned. Paul mentions Barnabas with honor in his writings, and in the very last of his epistles he sends for Mark to come to him at Rome, expressly adding that he is profitable to him for ministry—the very thing he had disbelieved about him before. In the meantime, however, their difference separated them. They agreed to divide between them the region they had evangelized together. Barnabas and Mark went to Cyprus; and Paul undertook to visit the churches on the mainland. As companion he took with him Silas, or Silvanus, in the place of Barnabas; and he had not gone far on his new journey when he met someone to take the place of Mark. This was Timothy, a convert he had made at Lystra on his first journey; he was youthful and gentle; and he continued a faithful companion and a constant comfort to the apostle to the end of his life.

92. In pursuing the purpose with which he had set out, Paul began this journey by revisiting the churches in the founding of which he had taken part. Beginning at Antioch and proceeding in a northwesterly direction, he did this work in Syria, Cilicia, and other places, until he reached the center of Asia Minor, where the primary object of his journey was completed. But, when a person is on the right road, all sorts of opportunities open up before him. When he had passed through the provinces he had visited before, new desires to penetrate still farther began to fire his mind, and Providence opened up the way.

He still went forward in the same direction through Phrygia and Galatia. Bithynia, a large province lying along the shore of the Black Sea, and Asia, a densely populated province in the west of Asia Minor, seemed to invite him and he wished to enter them. But the Spirit who guided his footsteps indicated, by some means unknown to us, that these provinces were shut to him for the present; and, pushing onward in the direction in which his divine Guide permitted him to go, he found himself at Troas, a town on the northwest coast of Asia Minor.

93. Thus he had traveled from Antioch in the southeast to Troas in the northwest of Asia Minor, evangelizing all the way. It must have taken months, perhaps even years. Yet of this long, laborious period we possess no details whatever, except such features of his intercourse with the Galatians as may be gathered from the epistle to that church. The truth is that, thrilling as are the notices of Paul's career given in the Book of Acts, this record is a very meager and imperfect one, and his life was far fuller of adventure, of labors and sufferings for Christ, than even Luke's narrative would lead us to suppose. The plan of the Acts is to tell only what was most novel and characteristic in each journey, while it passes over, for instance, all his repeated visits to the same scenes. There are thus great blanks in the history, which were in reality as full of interest as the portions of his life that are fully described.

Of this there is a startling proof in an epistle that he wrote within the period covered by the Acts of the Apostles. His argument calling on him to enumerate some of his outstanding adventures, "Are they ministers of Christ?" he asks, "I am more; in labors more abundant, in stripes above measure, in prisons more frequent; in deaths oft. Of the Jews five times received I forty stripes save one. Thrice was I beaten with rods. Once was I stoned. Thrice I suffered shipwreck. A night and a day have I been in the deep. In journeyings often, in perils of water, in perils of robbers, in perils by mine own countrymen, in perils by the heathen, in perils in the city, in perils in the wilderness, in perils in the sea, in perils among false brethren; in weariness and painfulness, in watchings often, in hunger and thirst, in fastings often, in cold and nakedness."

Now, of the items of this extraordinary catalog the Book of Acts mentions very few: of the five Jewish scourgings it notices not one, of the three Roman beatings only one; the one stoning it records, but not one of the three shipwrecks, for the shipwreck so fully detailed in the Acts happened later. It was no part of the design of Luke to exaggerate the figure of the hero he was painting; his brief and modest narrative comes far short even of the reality; and, as we pass over the few simple words into which he condenses the story of months or years, our imagination requires to be busy, filling up the outline with toils and pains at least equal to those the memory of which he has preserved.

94. It would appear that Paul reached Troas under the direction of the guiding Spirit without being aware where his steps were next to be turned. But could he doubt what the divine intention was when, gazing across the silver streak of the Hellespont, he beheld the shores of Europe on the other side? He was now within the charmed circle where for ages civilization had had her home; and he could not be entirely ignorant of those stories of war and enterprise and those legends of love and valor that have made it forever bright and dear to the heart of mankind.

At only four miles' distance lay the Plain of Troy, where Europe and Asia encountered each other in the struggle celebrated in Homer's immortal song. Not far away Xerxes, sitting on a marble throne, reviewed the three million Asiatics with which he meant to bring Europe to his feet. On the other side of that narrow strait lay Greece and Rome, the centers from which issued the learning, the commerce, and the armies that governed the world. Could his heart, so ambitious for the glory of Christ, fail to be fired with the desire to cast himself on these strongholds, or could he doubt that the Spirit was leading him forward to this enterprise? He knew that Greece, with all her wisdom, lacked that knowledge that makes wise unto salvation, and that the Romans, though they were the conquerors of this world, did not know the way of winning an inheritance in the world that is to come; but in his breast he carried the secret they both required.

95. It may have been such thoughts, dimly moving in his mind, that projected themselves into the vision he saw at Troas; or was it the vision that first awakened the idea of crossing to Europe? As he lay asleep, with the murmur of the Aegean in his ears, he saw a man standing on the opposite coast, on which he had been looking before he went to rest, calling and crying, "Come over into Macedonia and help us." That figure represented Europe, and its cry for help Europe's need of Christ. Paul recognized in it a divine summons; and the very next sunset that bathed the Hellespont in its golden light shown on his figure seated on the deck of a ship the prow of which was moving toward the shore of Macedonia.

96. In this passage of Paul, from Asia to Europe, a great providential decision was taking effect, of which, as children of the West, we cannot think without the profoundest thankfulness. Christianity arose in Asia and among an Oriental people; and it might have been expected to spread first among those races to which the Jews were most closely related. Instead of coming west, it might have gone eastward. It might have penetrated into Arabia and taken possession of those regions where the faith of the false prophet now holds sway. It might have visited the wandering tribes of Central Asia and, piercing its way down through the passes of the Himalayas, reared its temples on the banks of the Ganges, the Indus, and the Godavari. It might have traveled farther east to deliver the swarming millions of China from the cold secularism of Confucius. Had it done so, missionaries from India and Japan might have been coming to England and America today to tell the story of the Cross. But Providence conferred on Europe a blessed priority, and the fate of our continent was decided when Paul crossed the Aegean.

97. As Greece lay nearer than Rome to the shore of Asia, its conquest for Christ was the great achievement of his second missionary journey. Like the rest of the world it was at that time under the sway of Rome, and the Romans had divided it into two provinces—Macedonia in the north and Achaia in the south. Macedonia was therefore the first scene of Paul's Greek mission. It was connected from east to west by a great Roman road, along which the missionary moved, and the places where we have accounts of his labors are Philippi, Thessalonica, and Beroea.

98. The Greek character in this northern province was much less corrupted than in the more polished society to the south. In the Macedonian population there still lingered something of the vigor and courage which four centuries before had made its soldiers the conquerors of the world. The churches that Paul founded here gave him more comfort than any he established elsewhere. None of his Epistles are more cheerful and cordial than those to the Thessalonians and the Philippians; and, as he wrote the latter late in life, the perseverance of the Macedonians in adhering to the gospel must have been as remarkable as the welcome they gave it at first. At Beroea he even met with a generous and openminded synagogue of Jews— the most unusual occurence in his experience.

99. A prominent feature of the work in Macedonia was the part taken in it by women. Amid the general decay of religions throughout the world at this period, many women everywhere sought satisfaction for their religious instincts in the pure faith of the synagogue. In Macedonia, perhaps on account of its sound morality, these female proselytes were more numerous than elsewhere; and they pressed in large numbers into the Christian church. This was a good omen; it was a prophecy of the happy change in the lot of women which Christianity was to produce in the nations of the West. If man owes much to Christ, woman owes still more. He has delivered her from the degradation of being man's slave and plaything and raised her to be his friend and his equal before heaven; while, on the other hand, a new glory has been added to Christ's religion by the elegance and dignity with which it is invested when embodied in the female character.

These things were vividly illustrated in the earliest footsteps of Christianity on our continent. The first convert in Europe was a woman, at the first Christian service held on European soil the heart of Lydia being opened to receive the truth; and the change that took place in her prefigured what woman in Europe was to become under the influence of Christianity. In the same town of Philippi there was seen at the same time an equally representative image of the condition of woman in Europe before the gospel reached it, in a poor girl, possessed of a spirit of divination and held in slavery by men who were making gain out of her misfortune. Paul restored her to sanity.

Her misery and degradation were a symbol of the disfiguration, as Lydia's sweet and benevolent Christian character was of the transfiguration of womanhood.

100. Another feature that prominently marked the Macedonian churches was a spirit of liberality. They insisted on supplying the bodily wants of the missionaries; and, even after Paul had left them, they sent gifts to meet his necessities in other towns. Long afterward, when he was a prisoner at Rome, they commissioned Epaphroditus, one of their teachers, to carry similar gifts to him and to act as his attendant. Paul accepted the generosity of these loyal hearts, though in other places he would work his fingers to the bone and forego his natural rest rather than accept similar favors. Nor was their willingness to give due to superior wealth. On the contrary, they gave out of deep poverty. They were poor to begin with, and they were made poorer by the persecutions they had to endure. These were very severe after Paul left, and they lasted long. Of course, they had broken first of all on Paul himself. Though he was so successful in Macedonia, he was swept out of every town at last like the offscourings of all things. It was generally by the Jews that this was brought about. They either fanaticized the mob against him, or accused him before the Roman authorities of introducing a new religion or disturbing the peace or proclaiming a king who would be a rival to Caesar. They would neither go into the kingdom of heaven themselves nor allow others to enter.

101. But God protected His servant. At Philippi He delivered him from prison by a physical miracle and by a miracle of grace still more marvelous performed in his cruel jailor; and in other towns He saved him by more natural means. In spite of bitter opposition, churches were founded in city after city, and from these the glad tidings sounded out over the whole province of Macedonia.

102. When, leaving Macedonia, Paul proceeded south into Achaia, he entered the real Greece—the paradise of genius and renown. The memorials of the country's greatness rose around him on his journey. As he left Beroea, he could see behind him the snowy peaks of Mount Olympus, where the deities of Greece were supposed to dwell. Soon he was sailing past Thermopylae, where the immortal Three Hundred stood against the barbarian myriads; and, as his voyage neared its end, he saw before him the island of Salamis, where again the existence of Greece was saved from extinction by the valor of her sons.

103. His destination was Athens, the capital of the country. As he entered the city, he could not be insensible to the great memories that clung to its streets and monuments. Here the human mind had blazed forth with a splendor it has never exhibited elsewhere. In the golden age of its history Athens possessed more men of the highest genius than have ever lived in any other city. To this day their names invest it with glory. Yet even in Paul's day the living Athens was a thing of the past. Four hundred years had elapsed since its golden age, and in the course of these centuries it had experienced a sad decline. Philosophy had degenerated into sophistry, art into amateurism, oratory into rhetoric, poetry into versemaking. It was a city living on its past. Yet it still had a great name and was full of culture and learning of a kind. It swarmed with so-called philosophers of different schools, and with teachers and professors of every variety of knowledge; and thousands of strangers of the wealthy class, collected from all parts of the world, lived there for study or the gratification of their intellectual tastes. It still represented to an intelligent visitor one of the great factors in the life of the world.

104. With the amazing versatility that enabled him to be all things to all men, Paul adapted himself to this population also. In the marketplace, the lounge of the learned, he entered into conversation with students and philosophers, as Socrates had been accustomed to do on the same spot five centuries before. But he found even less appetite for the truth than the wisest of the Greeks had met with. Instead of the love of truth an insatiable intellectual curiosity possessed the inhabitants. This made them willing enough to tolerate the advances of anyone bringing before them a new doctrine; and, as long as Paul was merely developing the speculative part of his message, they listened to him with pleasure. Their interest seemed to deepen, and at last a multitude of them conveyed him to Mars' Hill, in the very center of the splendors of their city, and requested a full statement of his faith. He complied with their wishes and in the magnificent speech he made there, gratified their peculiar tastes to the full, as in sentences of the noblest eloquence he unfolded the great truths of the unity of God and the unity of man, which lie at the foundation of Christianity. But, when he advanced from these preliminaries to touch the consciences of his audience and address them about their own salvation, they departed in a body and left him talking.

105. He left Athens and never returned to it. Nowhere else had he so completely failed. He had been accustomed to endure the most violent persecution and to rally from it with a light heart. But there is something worse than persecution to a fiery faith like his, and he had to encounter it here: his message roused neither interest nor opposition. The Athenians never thought of persecuting him; they simply did not care what the babbler said; and this cold disdain cut him more deeply than the stones of the mob or the lictors' rods. Never perhaps was he so depressed. When he left Athens, he moved on to Corinth, the other great city of Achaia; and he tells us himself that he arrived there in weakness and in fear and in much trembling.

106. There was in Corinth enough of the spirit of Athens to prevent these feelings from being easily assuaged. Corinth was to Athens very much what Glasgow is to Edinburgh. The one was the commercial, the other the intellectual capital of the country. Even the situations of the two places in Greece resembled in some respects those of these two cities in Scotland. But the Corinthians also were full of argumentative curiosity and intellectual haughtiness. Paul dreaded the same kind of reception he had met with in Athens. Could it be that these were people for whom the gospel had no message? This was the staggering question that was making him tremble. There seemed to be nothing in them on which the gospel could take hold: they appeared to feel no wants that it could satisfy.

107. There were other elements of discouragement in Corinth. It was the Paris of ancient times—a city rich and luxurious, wholly abandoned to sensuality. Vice displayed itself without shame in forms that struck deadly despair into Paul's pure Jewish mind. Could men be rescued from the grasp of such monstrous vices? Besides, the opposition of the Jews rose here to unusual virulence. He was compelled at length to depart from the synagogue altogether, and did so with expressions of strong feeling. Was the soldier of Christ going to be driven off the field and forced to confess that the gospel was not suited for cultured Greece? It looked like it.

108. But the tide turned. At the critical moment Paul was visited with one of those visions that had a tendency to come to him at the most trying and decisive crises of his history. The Lord appeared to him in the night, saying, "Be not afraid, but speak, and hold not thy peace; for I am with thee, and no man shall set on thee to hurt thee; for I have much people in this city." The apostle took courage again, and the causes of discouragement began to clear away. The opposition of the Jews was broken, when they hurried him with mob violence before the Roman governor, Gallio, but were dismissed from the tribunal with ignominy and disdain. The president of the synagogue became a Christian, and conversions multiplied among the native Corinthians. Paul enjoyed the solace of living under the roof of two loyal-hearted friends of his own race and his own occupation, Aquila and Priscilla. He remained a year and a half in the city and founded one of the most interesting of his churches, thus planting the standard of the cross in Achaia also and proving that the gospel is the power of God to salvation even in the headquarters of the world's wisdom.

THE THIRD JOURNEY

109. It must have been a thrilling story Paul had to tell at Jerusalem and Antioch when he returned from his second journey; but he had no disposition to rest on his laurels, and it was not long before he set out on his third journey.

110. It might have been expected that, having in his second journey planted the gospel in Greece, he would in his third have made Rome his principal aim. But, if the map is referred to, it will be observed that, in the midst, between the regions of Asia Minor which he evangelized during his first journey and the provinces of Greece in which he planted churches in his second journey, there was a hiatus—the populous province of Asia, in the west of Asia Minor. It was in this region that he came on his third journey. Staying for no less than three years in Ephesus, its capital, he effectively filled up the gap and connected together the conquests of his former campaigns. This journey included at its beginning a visitation of all the churches formerly founded in Asia Minor and, at its close, a flying visit to the churches of Greece; but, true to his plan of dwelling only on what was new in each journey, the author of the Acts has supplied us only with the details relating to Ephesus.

111. This city was at that time the Liverpool of the Mediterranean. It possessed a splendid harbor, in which was concentrated the traffic of the sea that was then the highway of the nations; and, as Liverpool has behind her the great towns of Lancashire, so had Ephesus behind and around her such cities as those mentioned along with her in the epistles to the churches in the Book of Revelation—Smyrna, Pergamos, Thyatira, Sardis, Philadelphia, and Laodicea. It was a city of vast wealth, and it was given over to every kind of pleasure, the fame of its theater and race course being world-wide.

112. But Ephesus was still more famous as a sacred city. It was a seat of the worship of the goddess Diana, whose temple was one of the most celebrated shrines of the ancient world. This temple was enormously rich and harbored great numbers of priests. At certain seasons of the year it was a resort for flocks of pilgrims from the surrounding regions; and the inhabitants of the town flourished by ministering in various ways to this superstition. The goldsmiths drove a trade in little silver models of the image of the goddess that the temple contained and which was said to have fallen from heaven. Copies of the mystic characters engraved on this ancient relic were sold as charms. The city swarmed with wizards, fortune-tellers, interpreters of dreams, and other gentry of the like kind, who traded on the mariners, merchants, and pilgrims who frequented the port.

113. Paul's work had therefore to assume the form of a polemic against superstition. He performed such astonishing miracles in the name of Jesus that some of the Jewish tricksters with the invisible world attempted to cast out devils by invoking the same name; but the attempt resulted in their notable discomfiture. Other professors of magical arts were converted to the Christian faith and burned their books. The vendors of superstitious objects saw their trade slipping through their fingers. To such an extent did this go at one of the festivals of the goddess that the silversmiths, whose traffic in little images had been especially smitten, organized a riot against Paul, which took place in the theater and was so successful that he was forced to leave the city.

114. But he did not go before Christianity was firmly established in Ephesus, and the beacon of the gospel was twinkling brightly on the Asian coast, in response to that which was shining from the shores of Greece on the other side ot the Aegean. We have a monument of his success in the churches lying all around Ephesus which St. John addressed a few years later in the Apocalypse; for they were probably the indirect fruit of Paul's labors. But we have a far more astonishing monument of it in the Epistle to the Ephesians. This is perhaps the profoundest book in existence; yet its author evidently expected the Ephesians to understand it. If the orations of Demosthenes, with their closely packed arguments between the articulations of which even a knife cannot be thrust, is a monument of the intellectual greatness of the Greece that listened to them with pleasure; if the plays of Shakespeare, with their deep views of life and their obscure and complex language, be a testimony to the strength of mind of the Elizabethan Age, which could enjoy such solid fare in a place of entertainment; then the Epistle to the Ephesians, which sounds the lowest depths of Christian doctrine and scales the loftiest heights of Christian experience, is a testimony to the proficiency that Paul's converts had attained under his preaching in the capital of Asia.

7

HIS WRITINGS
AND HIS CHARACTER

PRINCIPAL LITERARY PERIOD

115. It has been mentioned that the third missionary journey closed with a flying visit to the churches of Greece. This visit lasted several months; but in the Acts it is passed over in two or three verses. It was probably little marked with those exciting incidents that naturally tempt the biographer into detail. Yet we know from other sources that it was nearly the most important part of Paul's life; for during this half year he wrote the greatest of all his Epistles, that to the Romans, and two others only less important—that to the Galatians and the Second to the Corinthians.

116. We have thus alighted on the portion of his life most marked by literary work. Overpowering as is the impression of the remarkableness of this man produced

89

by following him, as we have been doing, as he hurries from province to province, from continent to continent, over land and sea, in pursuit of the object to which he was devoted, this impression is immensely deepened when we remember that he was at the same time the greatest thinker of his age, if not of any age. Also, in the midst of his outward labors, he was producing writings that have ever since been among the mightiest intellectual forces of the world, and are still growing in their influence.

In this respect he rises high above all other evangelists and missionaries. Some of them may have approached him in certain respects—Xavier or Livingstone in the world-conquering instinct, St. Bernard or Whitefield in earnestness and activity. But few of these men added a single new idea to the world's stock of beliefs, whereas Paul, while at least equaling them in their own special line, gave to mankind a new world of thought. If his Epistles would perish, the loss to literature would be the greatest possible with only one exception—that of the Gospels, which record the life, the sayings, and the death of our Lord. They have quickened the mind of the church as no other writings have done, and have scattered in the soil of the world hundreds of seeds the fruits of which are now the general possession of mankind. Out of them have been brought the watchwords of progress in every reformation that the church has experienced. When Luther awoke Europe from the slumber of centuries, it was a word of Paul that he uttered with his mighty voice: and when, one hundred years ago, our own country was revived from almost universal spiritual death, she was called by the voices of men who had rediscovered the truth for themselves in the pages of Paul.

117. Yet in penning his Epistles Paul may himself have had little idea of the part they were to play in the future. They were drawn out of him simply by the exigencies of his work. In the truest sense of the word they were letters, written to meet particular occasions, not formal writings, carefully designed and executed with a view to fame or to futurity. Letters of the right kind are, before everything else, products of the heart; and it was the eager heart of Paul, yearning for the weal of his spiritual children or alarmed by the dangers to which they were exposed, that produced all his writings. They were part of his day's work. Just as he flew over sea and land to revisit his converts, or sent Timothy or Titus to carry them his counsels and bring news of how they fared, so, when these means were not available, he would send a letter with the same design.

118. This may seem to detract from the value of these writings. We may be inclined to wish that, instead of having the course of his thinking determined by the exigencies of so many special occasions and his attention distracted by so many minute particulars, he had been able to concentrate the force of his mind on one perfect book and expound his views on the high subjects that occupied his thoughts in a systematic form. It cannot be maintained that Paul's Epistles are models of style. They were written far too hurriedly for this; and the last thing he thought of was to polish his periods. Often, his ideas, by the mere virtue of their quality and beauty, run into forms of exquisite language, or there is in them such a sustained throb of emotion that they shape themselves spontaneously into sentences of noble eloquence. But more often his language is rugged and formless; no doubt it was the first that came to mind for expressing what he had to say. He begins sentences and doesn't finish them; he goes off into digressions and forgets to pick up the line of thought he has dropped; he throws out his ideas in lumps instead of fusing them into mutual coherence.

Nowhere perhaps will there be found so exact a

parallel to the style of Paul as in the letters and speeches of Oliver Cromwell. In the Protector's brain there lay the best and truest thoughts about England and her complicated affairs that existed at the time in that island; but, when he tried to express them in speech or letter, there came from his mind the most extraordinary mixture of exclamations, questions, arguments that soon became lost in the sands of words, unwieldy parentheses, and morsels of beautiful pathos or subduing eloquence. Yet, as you read these amazing utterances, you come by degrees to feel that you are getting to see the very heart and soul of the Puritan Era, and that you would rather be beside this man than any other representative of the period. You see the events and ideas of the time in the process of birth.

Perhaps, indeed, a certain formlessness is a natural accompaniment of the highest originality. The perfect expression and orderly arrangement of ideas is a later process; but, when great thoughts come forth for the first time, there is a kind of primordial roughness about them, as if the earth out of which they arise was still clinging to them: the polishing of the gold comes late and has to be preceded by the casting of the ore out of the bowels of nature. Paul in his writings hurls forth the original ore of truth. We owe to him hundreds of ideas that were never uttered before.

After the original man has his idea out, the most commonplace scribe may be able to express it for others better than he, though he could never have originated it. So throughout the writings of Paul there are thoughts that others may combine into systems of theology and ethics, and it is the duty of the church to do so. But his Epistles permit us to see revelation in the very process of birth. As we read them closely, we seem to be witnessing the creation of a world of truth, as the angels wondered to see the firmament evolving itself out of chaos and the multitudinous earth spreading itself forth in the light. Minute as are the details he often has to deal with, the whole of his vast view of the truth is recalled in his treatment of every one of them, as the whole sky is mirrored in a single drop of dew. What could be a more impressive proof of the fecundity of his mind than the fact that, amid the innumerable distractions of a second visit to his Greek converts, he should have written in half a year three books such as Romans, Galatians and Second Corinthians?

HIS INSPIRATION

119. It was God by His Spirit who communicated this revelation of truth to Paul. Its own greatness and divineness supply the best proof that it could have had no other origin. But none the less did it break in on Paul with the joy and pain of original thought; it came to him through his experience; it drenched and dyed every fiber of his mind and heart; and the expression that it found in his writings was in accordance with his peculiar genius and circumstances.

THE MAN REVEALED IN HIS LETTERS

120. It would be easy to suggest compensations in the form of Paul's writings for the literary qualities they lack. But one of these so outweighs all others that it is sufficient by itself to justify in this case the ways of God. In no other literary form could we, to the same extent in the writings, understand the man. Letters are the most personal form of literature. A man may write a treatise or a history or even a poem and hide his personality behind it; but letters are valueless unless the writer shows himself. Paul is constantly visible in his letters. You can feel his heart throbbing in every chapter he ever wrote. He has painted his own portrait—not only that of the outward man, but of his innermost feelings—as no one else could have painted it. It is not from Luke, admirable as is the picture drawn in the Acts of the Apostles, that we learn what the true Paul was, but from Paul himself. The truths he reveals are all seen embodied in the man. As there are some preachers who are greater than their sermons, and the principal gain of their hearers, in listening to them, is received in the inspiring glimpses they have of a great and sanctified personality, so the best thing in the writings of Paul is Paul himself, or rather the grace of God in him.

121. His character presented a wonderful combination of the natural and the spiritual. From nature he had received a strongly marked individuality; but the change that Christianity produces was no less obvious in him. In no saved man's character is it possible to separate completely what is due to nature from what is due to grace; for nature and grace blend sweetly in the redeemed life. In Paul the union of the two was singularly complete; yet it was always clear that there were two elements in him of diverse origin; and this is indeed the key to a successful estimate of his character.

PHYSIQUE

122. To begin with what was most simply natural— his physique was an important condition of his career. As a lack of a musical ear may make a musical career impossible or a failure of eyesight stop the progress of a painter, so the missionary life is impossible without a certain degree of physical stamina. To anyone reading by itself the catalog of Paul's sufferings and observing the elasticity with which he rallied from the severest of them and resumed his labors, it would naturally occur that he must have been a person of Herculean strength. On the contrary, he appears to have been little of stature, and his bodily presence was weak. This weakness seems to have been sometimes aggravated by disfiguring disease; and he felt keenly the disappointment that he knew his bodily presence would excite among strangers; for every preacher who loves his work would like to preach the gospel with all the graces that conciliate the favor of hearers to an orator. God, however, used his very weakness, beyond his hopes, to draw out the tenderness of his converts; and so, when he was weak, then he was strong, and he was able to glory even in his infirmities.

There is a theory that has gained much popularity, that the disease he suffered from was violent opthalmia, causing disagreeable redness of the eyelids. But grounds for this idea are very slender. He seems, on the contrary, to have had a remarkable power of fascinating and cowing an enemy with the sharpness of his glance, as in the story of Elymas the sorcerer, which reminds us of the tradition about Luther, that his eyes sometimes so glowed and sparkled that bystanders could scarcely look on them.

There is no foundation whatever for an idea of some recent biographers of Paul that his bodily constitution was excessively fragile and chronically afflicted with shattering nervous disease. No one could have gone through his labors or suffered the stoning, the scourgings, and other tortures he endured without having an exceptionally tough and sound constitution. It is true that he was sometimes worn out with illness and weakened by the acts of violence to which he was exposed; but the rapidity of his recovery on such occasions proves what a large fund of bodily force he had to draw upon. And who can doubt that, when his face was softened with tender love in beseeching men to be reconciled to God or lit up with enthusiasm in the delivery of his message, it must have possessed a noble beauty far above mere regularity of feature?

ENTERPRISE

123. There was a good deal that was natural in another element of his character on which much depended—his spirit of enterprise. There are many men who like to grow up where they are born; to have to change into new circumstances and make acquaintance with new people is intolerable to them. But there are others who have a kind of vagabondism in the blood; they are the persons intended by nature for emigrants and pioneers; and, if they take to the work of the ministry, they make the best missionaries.

In modern times no missionary has had this consecrated spirit of adventure in the same degree as that great Scotsman, David Livingstone. When he first went to Africa, he found the missionaries clustered in the south of the continent, just within the fringe of heathenism; they had their houses and gardens, their families, their small congregations of natives; and they were content. But he moved at once beyond the rest into the heart of heathenism, and dreams of more distant regions never ceased to haunt him, until at length he began his extraordinary tramps over thousands of miles where no missionary had ever been before; and, when death overtook him, he was still pressing ahead.

Paul's was a nature of the same type, full of courage and adventure. The unknown in the distance, instead of dismaying, drew him on. He could not bear to build on other men's foundations, but was constantly hastening to virgin soil, leaving churches behind for others to build up. He believed that, if he lit the lamp of the gospel here and there over vast areas, the light would spread in his absence by its own virtue. He liked to count the parties he had left behind him, but his watchword was ever Forward. In his dreams he saw men calling him to new countries; he always had a long unfulfilled program in his mind; and, as death approached, he was still thinking of journeys into the remotest corners of the known world.

INFLUENCE OVER MEN

124. Another element of his character near to the one just mentioned was his influence over men. To some it is painful to have to accost a stranger even on pressing business; and most men are only quite at home in their own setting—among men of the same class or profession as themselves. But the life he had chosen brought Paul into contact with men of every kind, and he constantly had to be introducing to strangers the business with which he was charged. He might be addressing a king or a consul one hour and a roomful of slaves or common soldiers the next. One day he had to speak in the synagogue of the Jews, another day among a crowd of Athenian philosophers, another day to the inhabitants of some provincial town far from the seats of culture. But he could adapt himself to every man and every audience. To the Jews he spoke as a rabbi out of the Old Testament Scriptures; to the Greeks he quoted the words of their own poets; and to the barbarians he talked of the God who gives rain from heaven and fruitful seasons, filling our hearts with food and gladness.

When a weak or insincere man attempts to be all things to all men, he ends by being nothing to anyone. But, living on this principle, Paul found entrance for the gospel everywhere, and at the same time won for himself the esteem and love of those to whom he stooped. If he was bitterly hated by enemies, there was never a man more intensely loved by his friends. They received him as an angel of God, or even as Jesus Christ Himself, and were ready to pluck out their eyes and give them to him. One church was jealous of another getting too much of him. When he was not able to pay a visit at the time he had promised, they were furious, as if he had done them a wrong. When he was parting from them, they wept sorrowfully, and fell on his neck and kissed him. Numbers of young men were continually around him, ready to go on his errands. It was the size of his manhood that was the secret of this fascination; for to a big nature all follow, feeling that in its neighborhood it is well with them.

UNSELFISHNESS

125. This popularity was partly due, however, to another quality that shone conspicuously in his character—the spirit of unselfishness. This is the rarest quality in human nature, and it is the most powerful of all in its influence on others, where it exists in purity and strength. Most men are so absorbed in their own interests and so naturally expect others to be the same that, if they see anyone who appears to have no interests of his own to serve but is willing to do as much for the sake of others as the generality do for themselves, they are at first incredulous, suspecting that he is only hiding his designs beneath the cloak of benevolence; but, if he stands the test and his unselfishness proves to be genuine, there is no limit to the homage they are prepared to pay him. As Paul appeared in country after country and city after city, he was at first a complete enigma to those whom he approached. They formed all sorts of conjectures as to his real character. Was it money he was seeking, or power, or something darker and less pure? His enemies never ceased to throw out such insinuations. But those who got near him and saw what kind of person he was, who knew that he refused money and worked with his hands day and night to keep himself above the suspicion of mercenary motives, who heard him pleading with them one by one in their homes and exhorting them with tears to a holy life, who saw the sustained personal interest he took in every one of them—these could not resist the proofs of his disinterestedness or deny him their affection.

There never was a man more unselfish; he had literally no interest of his own to live for. Without family ties, he poured all the affections of his big nature, which might have been given to wife and children, into the channels of his work. He compares his tenderness toward his converts to that of a nursing mother to her children; he pleads with them to remember that he is their father who has begotten them in the gospel. They are his glory and crown, his hope and joy and crown of rejoicing. Eager as he was for new conquests, he never lost his hold on those he had won. He could assure his churches that he prayed and gave thanks for them night and day, and he remembered his converts by name at the throne of grace. How could human nature resist disinterestedness like this? If Paul was a conqueror of the world, he conquered it by the power of love.

HIS MISSION

126. The two most distinctively Christian features of his character still have to be mentioned. One of these was the sense of having a divine mission to preach Christ, which he was bound to fulfill. Most men merely drift through life, and the work they do is determined by a hundred indifferent circumstances; they might as well be doing anything else, or they would prefer, if they could afford it, to be doing nothing at all. But, from the time when he became a Christian, Paul knew that he had a definite work to do; and the call he had received to it never ceased to ring like an alarm in his soul. "Woe is unto me if I preach not the gospel"; this was the impulse that drove him on. He felt that he had a world of new truths to utter and that the salvation of mankind depended on their utterance. He knew himself called to make Christ known to as many of his fellow creatures as his strongest exertions could enable him to reach. It was this that made him so impetuous in his movements, so blind to danger, so contemptuous of suffering. "None of these things move me, neither count I my life dear unto myself, so that I might finish my course with joy, and the ministry which I have received of the Lord Jesus, to testify the gospel of the grace of God." He lived with the account that he would have to give at the judgment seat of Christ always in his eye, and his heart was revived in every hour of discouragement by the vision of the crown of life which, if he proved faithful, the Lord, the righteous Judge, would place on his head.

DEVOTION TO CHRIST

127. The other uniquely Christian quality that shaped his career was personal devotion to Christ. This was the supreme characteristic of the man, and from first to last the mainspring of his activities. From the moment of his first meeting with Christ he had but one passion; his love to his Savior burned with more and more brightness to the end. He delighted to call himself the slave of Christ, and had no ambition except to be the propagator of His ideas and the continuance of His influence.

He took up this idea of being Christ's representative with startling boldness. He says the heart of Christ is beating in his bosom toward his converts; he says the mind of Christ is thinking in his brain; he says that he is continuing the work of Christ and filling up that which was lacking in His sufferings; he says the wounds of Christ are reproduced in the scars on his body; he says he is dying that others may live, as Christ died for the life of the world. But it was in reality the deepest humility that lay beneath these bold expressions. He had the sense that Christ had done everything for him; He had entered into him, casting out the old Paul and ending the old life, and had begotten a new man, with new designs, feelings, and activities. And it was his deepest longing that this process should go on and become complete—that his old self should vanish away, and that the new self, which Christ had created in His own image and still sustained, should become so predominant that, when the thoughts of his mind were Christ's thoughts, the words on his lips Christ's words, the deeds he did Christ's deeds, and the character he wore Christ's character, he might be able to say, "I live, yet not I, but Christ liveth in me."

8

PICTURE OF A PAULINE CHURCH

HISTORY WITHOUT AND WITHIN

128. A holiday visitor to a foreign city walks through the streets, guidebook in hand, looking at monuments, churches, public buildings, and the outsides of the houses, and in this way is supposed to become acquainted with the town; but, on reflection, he will find that he has scarcely learned anything about it, because he has not been inside the houses. He does not know how the people live—not even what kind of furniture they have or what kind of food they eat—not to speak of far deeper matters, such as how they love, what they admire and pursue, and whether they are content with their lot.

In reading history one is often at a loss in the same way. It is only the outside of life that is made visible. It is as if the eye were carried along the external surface of a tree, instead of seeing a cross section of its substance. The pomp and glitter of the court, the wars waged and the victories won, the changes in the constitution and the rise and fall of administrations, are faithfully recorded; but the reader feels that he would learn far more of the real history of the time if he could see for one hour what was happening beneath the roofs of the peasant, the shopkeeper, the clergyman, and the noble.

Even in Scripture history there is the same difficulty. In the narrative of the Acts of the Apostles we receive thrilling accounts of the external details of Paul's history; we are carried rapidly from city to city and informed of the incidents that accompanied the founding of the various churches; but we cannot help wishing sometimes to stop and learn what one of these churches was like inside. In Paphos or Iconium, in Thessalonica or Beroea or Corinth, how did things continue after Paul left? What were the Christians like, and what was the aspect of their worship?

129. Happily it is possible to obtain this interior view of things. As Luke's narrative describes the outside of Paul's career, so Paul's own Epistles permit us to see its deeper aspects. They rewrite the history on a different plane. This is especially the case with those Epistles written at the close of his third journey, which cast a flood of light back on the period covered by all his journeys. In addition to the three Epistles already mentioned as having been written at this time, there is another belonging to the same part of his life—the First to the Corinthians —which may be said to transport us, as on a magician's mantle, back over two thousand years and, stationing us in midair above a great Greek city, in which there was a Christian church, to take the roof off the meeting house of the Christians and permit us to see what was going on within.

A CHRISTIAN GATHERING IN CORINTH

130. It is a strange spectacle we witness from this vantage point. It is Sabbath evening, but of course the heathen city knows of no Sabbath. The day's work at the busy seaport is over, and the streets are thronged with revelers intent on a night of pleasure, for it is the wickedest city of that wicked ancient world. Hundreds of merchants and sailors from foreign parts are lounging about. The frivolous young Roman, who has come across to this Paris for a bout of dissipation, drives his light chariot through the streets. If it is near the time of the annual games, there are groups of boxers, runners, charioteers, and wrestlers, surrounded by their admirers and discussing their chances of winning the coveted crowns. In the warm genial climate old and young are out of doors enjoying the evening hour, while the sun, going down over the Adriatic, is casting its golden light on the palaces and temples of the wealthy city.

131. Meanwhile, the little company of Christians has been gathering from all directions to their place of worship, for it is the hour of their stated assembly. The place of meeting itself does not rise clearly before our view. But at all events it is no gorgeous temple like those by which it is surrounded; it has not even the pretensions of the neighboring synagogue. It may be a large room in a private house or the wareroom of some Christian merchant cleared for the occasion.

132. Glance around the benches and look at the faces. You at once discern one marked distinction among them: some have the peculiar facial contour of the Jew, while the rest are Gentiles of various nationalities; and the latter are the majority. But look closer still and you notice another distinction: some wear the ring that denotes that they are free, while others are slaves; and the latter preponderate. Here and there among the gentile members there is one with the regular features of the born Greek, perhaps shaded with the pale thoughtfulness of the philosopher or distinguished with the self-confidence of wealth; but not many great, not many mighty, not many noble are there; the majority belong to what in this pretentious city would be considered the foolish, the weak, the base and despised things of this world; they are slaves, whose ancestors did not breathe the clear air of Greece but roamed in savage hordes on the banks of the Danube or the Don.

133. But observe one thing besides on all the faces present—the terrible traces of their past life. In a modern Christian congregation one sees in the faces on every hand that peculiar cast of feature that Christian nurture, inherited through many centuries, has produced; and it is only here and there that a face may be seen in the lines of which is written the tale of debauchery or crime. But in this Corinthian congregation these awful hieroglyphics are everywhere. "Know ye not," Paul writes to them, "that the unrighteous shall not inherit the kingdom of God? Be not deceived: neither fornicators, nor idolaters, nor adulterers, nor effeminate, nor abusers of themselves with mankind, nor thieves, nor covetous, nor extortioners shall inherit the kingdom of God. And such were some of you." Look at that tall, sallow-faced Greek: he once wallowed in the mire of Circe's swine pens. Look at that low-browed Scythian slave: he had been a pickpocket and a prisoner. Look at that thin-nosed, sharp-eyed Jew: he had been a Shylock, cutting his pound of flesh from the gilded youth of Corinth.

Yet there has been a great change. Another story besides the tale of sin is written on these countenances. "But ye are washed, but ye are sanctified, but ye are justified in the name of the Lord Jesus and by the Spirit of our God." Listen, they are singing; it is the fortieth Psalm: "He took me from the fearful pit and from the miry clay." What pathos they throw into the words, what joy overspreads their faces! They know themselves to be monuments of free grace and dying love.

THE SERVICES

134. But suppose they are now all gathered for worship; how does their worship proceed? There was this difference between their services and most of ours, that instead of one man conducting them—offering their prayers, preaching, and reading the psalms—all the men present were at liberty to contribute their part. There may have been a leader or chairman; but one member might read a portion of Scripture, another offer a prayer, a third deliver an address, a fourth suggest a hymn, and so on. Nor does there seem to have been any fixed order in which the different parts of the service occurred; any member might rise and lead the company into praise or prayer or meditation, as he felt prompted.

135. This peculiarity was due to another great difference between them and us. The members were endowed with very extraordinary gifts. Some of them had the power of working miracles, such as the healing of the sick. Others possessed a strange gift called the gift of tongues. It is not quite clear what it was; but it seems to have been a kind of tranced utterance, in which the speaker poured out an impassioned rhapsody by which his religious feeling received both expression and exaltation. Some who possessed this gift were not able to tell others the meaning of what they were saying, while others had this additional power; and there were those who, though not speaking with tongues themselves, were able to interpret what the inspired speakers were saying. Then again, there were members who possessed the gift of prophecy—a very valuable endowment. It was not the power of predicting future events, but a gift of impassioned eloquence, the effects of which were sometimes marvelous. When an unbeliever entered the assembly and listened to the prophets, he was seized with uncontrollable emotion, the sins of his past life would rise up before him, and, falling on his face, he would confess that God was truly among them. Other members exercised gifts more like those we are ourselves acquainted with, such as the gift of teaching or the gift of management. But in all cases there appears to have been a kind of immediate inspiration, so that what they did was not the effect of calculation or preparation, but of a strong present impulse.

136. These phenomena are so remarkable that, if narrated in a history, they would put a severe strain on belief. But the evidence for them is incontrovertible; for no man, writing to people about their own condition, invents a mythical description of their circumstances; and besides, Paul was writing to restrain rather than encourage these manifestations. They show with what mighty force, at its first entrance into the world, Christianity took possession of the spirits it touched. Each believer received, generally at his baptism, when the hands of the baptizer were laid on him, his special gift, which, if he remained faithful to it, he continued to exercise. It was the Holy Spirit, poured forth without limit, that entered into the spirits of men and distributed these gifts among them as He willed; and each member had to make use of his gift for the benefit of the whole body.

137. After the services just described were over, the members sat down to a love feast, which concluded with the breaking of bread in the Lord's Supper; and then, after a fraternal kiss, they parted to their homes. It was a memorable scene, radiant with brotherly love and alive with outbreaking spiritual power. As the Christians wended their way homeward through the careless groups of the heathen city, they were conscious of having experienced that which eye had not seen nor ear heard.

ABUSES AND IRREGULARITIES

138. But truth demands that the dark side of the picture be shown as well as the bright one. There were abuses and irregularities in the church that are exceedingly painful to recall. These were due to two things—the antecedents of the members and the mixture in the church of Jewish and gentile elements. If we can remember how vast was the change most of the members had made in passing from the worship of the heathen temples to the pure and simple worship of Christianity, it will not cause surprise that their old life still clung to them or that they did not clearly distinguish which things needed to be changed and which might continue as they had been.

139. Yet it startles us to learn that some of them were living in gross sensuality, and that the more philosophical defended this on principle. One member, apparently a person of wealth and position, was openly living in a relationship that would have been a scandal even among heathens, and, though Paul had indignantly written to have him excommunicated, the church had failed to obey, choosing to misunderstand the order. Others had been allured back to take part in the feasts in the idol temples, notwithstanding their accompaniments of drunkenness and revelry. They excused themselves with the plea that they no longer ate the feast in honor of the gods, but only as an ordinary meal, and argued that they would have to go out of the world if they were not at times to associate with sinners.

140. It is evident that these abuses belonged to the gentile section of the church. In the Jewish section, on the other hand, there were strange doubts and scruples about the same subjects. Some, for instance, revolted against the loose behavior of their gentile brethren, and had gone to the opposite extreme, denouncing marriage altogether and raising anxious questions as to whether widows might marry again, whether a Christian married to a heathen wife ought to put her away, and other points of the same nature. While some of the gentile converts were participating in the idol feasts, some of the Jewish members had scruples about buying in the market the meat that had been offered in sacrifice to idols, and looked with censure on their brethren who allowed themselves this freedom.

141. These difficulties belonged to the domestic life of the Christians; but, in their public meetings also, there were grave irregularities. The very gifts of the Spirit were perverted into instruments of sin; for many who possessed the more showy gifts, such as miracles and tongues, were too fond of displaying them, and turned them into grounds of boasting. This led to confusion and even uproar; for sometimes two or three who spoke with tongues would be pouring forth their unintelligible utterances at once, so that, as Paul said, if any stranger had entered their meeting, he would have concluded that they were all mad. The prophets spoke at wearisome length, and too many pressed forward to take part in the services. Paul sternly had to rebuke these extravagances, insisting on the principle that the spirits of the prophets were subject to the prophets, and that therefore the spiritual impulse was no apology for disorder.

142. But there were still worse things inside the church. Even the sacredness of the Lord's Supper was profaned. It seems that the members were in the habit of taking with them to church the bread and wine that were needed for this sacrament; but the wealthy brought abundant and choice supplies, and, instead of waiting for their poorer brethren and sharing their provisions with them, began to eat and drink so gluttonously that the table of the Lord actually resounded with drunkenness and riot.

143. One more dark touch must be added to this sad picture. In spite of the brotherly kiss with which their meetings closed, they had fallen into mutual rivalry and contention. No doubt this was due to the heterogeneous elements brought together in the church; but it had been allowed to go to great lengths. Brother went to law against brother in the heathen courts instead of seeking the arbitration of a Christian friend. The body of the members was split up into four theological factions. Some called themselves after Paul himself. These treated the scruples of the weaker brethren about meats and other things with scorn. Others took the name, Apollonians, from Apollos, an eloquent teacher from Alexandria, who visited Corinth between Paul's second and third journeys. These were the philosophical party; they denied the doctrine of the Resurrection, because it was absurd to suppose that the scattered atoms of the dead body could ever be united again. The third party took the name of Peter, or Cephas, as in their Hebrew purism they preferred to call him. These were narrow-minded Jews, who objected to the liberality of Paul's views. The fourth party sought to be above all parties and called themselves simply Christians. Like many despisers of the sects since then, who have used the name of Christian in the same way, these were the most bitterly sectarian of all and rejected Paul's authority with malicious scorn.

INFERENCES

144. Such is the checkered picture of one of Paul's churches given in one of his own Epistles; and it shows several things with much impressiveness. It shows, for instance, how exceptional, even in that age, his own mind and character were, and what a blessing his gifts and graces of good sense, of large sympathy blended with conscientious firmness, of personal purity and honor, were to the infant church. It shows that it is not behind but ahead that we have to look for the golden age of Christianity. It shows how perilous it is to assume that the prevalence of any ecclesiastical usage at that time must constitute a rule for all times. Everything of this kind was evidently at the experimental stage. Indeed, in the latest writings of Paul we find the picture of a very different state of things, in which the worship and discipline of the church were far more fixed and orderly. It is not for a pattern of the machinery of a church we ought to go back to this early time, but for a spectacle of fresh and trans- forming spiritual power. This is what will always attract to the Apostolic Age the longing eyes of Christians; the power of the Spirit was energizing in every member, the tides of fresh emotion swelled in every breast, and all felt that the dayspring of a new revelation had visited them; life, love, light were diffusing themselves everywhere. Even the vices of the young church were the irregularities of abundant life, for the lack of which the lifeless order of many a subsequent generation has been a poor compen- sation.

9

HIS GREAT CONTROVERSY

145. The version of the apostle's life supplied in his own letters is largely occupied with a controversy that cost him much pain and took up much of his time for many years, but of which Luke says little. At the date when Luke wrote, it was a dead controversy, and it belonged to a different plane from that along which his story moves. But at the time when it was raging, it tried Paul far more than tiresome journeys or angry seas. It was at its hottest about the close of his third journey, and the Epistles already mentioned as having been written then may be said to have been evoked by it. The Epistle to the Galatians especially was a thunderbolt hurled against his opponents in this controversy; and its burning sentences show how profoundly he was moved by the subject.

THE QUESTION AT ISSUE

146. The question at issue was whether the Gentiles were required to become Jews before they could be true

Christians; or, in other words, whether they had to be circumcised in order to be saved.

147. It had pleased God in primitive times to choose the Jewish race from among the nations and make it the repository of salvation; and, until the advent of Christ, those from other nations who wished to become partakers of the true religion had to seek entrance as proselytes within the sacred enclosure of Israel. Having thus destined this race to be the guardians of revelation, God had to separate them completely from all other nations and from all other purposes which might have distracted their attention from the sacred trust that had been committed to them. For this purpose He regulated their entire life with rules and arrangements intended to make them a peculiar people, different from all other races of the earth. Every detail of their life—their forms of worship, their social customs, their dress, their food—was prescribed for them; and all these prescriptions were embodied in that vast legal instrument they called the Law. The rigorous prescription of so many things that are naturally left to free choice was a heavy yoke on the chosen people; it was a severe discipline to the conscience, and such it was felt to be by the more earnest spirits of the nation.

But others saw in it a badge of pride; it made them feel that they were the select of the earth and superior to all other people; and, instead of groaning under the yoke, as they would have done if their consciences had been tender, they multiplied the distinctions of the Jew, swelling the volume of the prescriptions of the Law with stereotyped customs of their own. To be a Jew appeared to them the mark of belonging to the aristocracy of the nations; to be admitted to the privileges of this position was in their eyes the greatest honor that could be conferred on one who did not belong to the commonwealth of Israel. Their thoughts were all wound up within the circle of this national conceit. Even their hopes about the Messiah were colored with these prejudices; they expected Him to be the hero of their own nation, and the extension of His kingdom they conceived as a crowding of the other nations within the circle of their own through the gateway of circumcision. They expected that all the converts of the Messiah would undergo this national rite and adopt the life prescribed in the Jewish law and tradition; in short, their conception of Messiah's reign was a world of Jews.

148. Such undoubtedly was the tenor of popular sentiment in Palestine when Christ came; and multitudes who accepted Jesus as the Messiah and entered the Christian church had this set of conceptions as their intellectual horizon. They had become Christians, but they had not ceased to be Jews; they still attended the temple worship; they prayed at the stated hours, they fasted on the stated days, they dressed in the style of the Jewish ritual; they would have thought themselves defiled by eating with uncircumcised Gentiles; and they had no thought but that, if Gentiles became Christians, they would be circumcised and adopt the style and customs of the Jewish nation.

THE SETTLEMENT

149. The question was settled by the direct intervention of God in the case of Cornelius, the centurion of Caesarea. When the messengers of Cornelius were on their way to the apostle Peter at Joppa, God showed that leader among the apostles, by the vision of the sheet full of clean and unclean beasts, that the Christian church was to contain circumcised and uncircumcised alike. In obedience to this heavenly sign Peter accompanied the centurion's messengers to Caesarea and saw such evidences that the household of Cornelius had already, without circumcision, received the distinctively Christian endowments of faith and the Holy Spirit, that he could not hesitate to baptize them as being Christians already. When he returned to Jerusalem, his proceedings created wonder and indignation among the Christians of the strictly Jewish persuasion; but he defended himself by recounting the vision of the sheet and by an appeal to the clear fact that these uncircumcised Gentiles were proved by their possession of faith and of the Holy Spirit to have already been Christians.

150. This incident ought to have settled the question once for all; but the pride of race and the prejudices of a lifetime are not easily subdued. Although the Christians of Jerusalem reconciled themselves to Peter's conduct in this single case, they neglected to extract from it the universal principle that it implied; and even Peter himself, as we shall subsequently see, did not fully comprehend what was involved in his own conduct.

151. Meanwhile, however, the question had been settled in a far stronger and more logical mind than Peter's. Paul at this time began his apostolic work at Antioch, and soon afterward went forth with Barnabas on his first great missionary expedition into the Gentile world; and, wherever they went, he admitted heathens into the Christian church without circumcision.

Paul in this acting did not copy Peter. He had received his gospel directly from heaven. In the solitudes of Arabia, in the years immediately after his conversion, he had thought this subject out and had come to far more radical conclusions about it than had yet entered the minds of any of the rest of the apostles. To him far more than to any of them the Law had been a yoke of bondage; he saw that it was only a stern preparation for Christianity, not a part of it; indeed, there was in his mind a

deep gulf of contrast between the misery and curse of the one state and the joy and freedom of the other. To his mind to impose the yoke of the Law on the Gentiles would have been to destroy the very genius of Christianity; it would have been the imposition of conditions of salvation totally different from that which he knew to be the one condition of it in the gospel.

These were the deep reasons that settled this question in this great mind. Besides, as a man who knew the world and whose heart was set on winning the gentile nations to Christ, he felt far more strongly than did the Jews of Jerusalem, with their provincial horizon, how fatal such conditions as they meant to impose would be to the success of Christianity outside Judaea. The proud Romans, the highminded Greeks, would never have consented to be circumcised and to cramp their life within the narrow limits of Jewish tradition; a religion hampered with such conditions could never have become the universal religion.

152. But, when Paul and Barnabas came back from their first missionary tour to Antioch, they found that a still more decisive settlement of this question was required; for Christians of the strictly Jewish type were coming down from Jerusalem to Antioch and telling the gentile converts that, unless they were circumcised, they could not be saved. In this way they were filling them with alarm, lest they might be omitting something on which the welfare of their souls depended, and they were confusing their minds as to the simplicity of the gospel. To quiet these disturbed consciences it was resolved by the church at Antioch to appeal to the leading apostles at Jerusalem, and Paul and Barnabas were sent there to procure a decision. This was the origin of what is called the Council of Jerusalem, at which this question was authoritatively settled.

The decision of the apostles and elders was in harmony with Paul's practice: the Gentiles were not to be required to be circumcised; only they were required to abstain from meat offered in sacrifice to idols, from fornication, and from blood. To these conditions Paul consented. He did not see any harm in eating meat that had been used in idolatrous sacrifices, when it was exposed for sale in the market; but the feasts using such meat in the idol temples, which were often followed by wild outbreaks of sensuality, alluded to in the prohibition of fornication, were temptations against which the converts from heathenism needed to be warned. The prohibition of blood—that is, of eating meat killed without the blood being drained off—was a concession to extreme Jewish prejudice, which, as it involved no principle, he did not think it necessary to oppose.

153. So the agitating question appeared to be settled by an authority so august that none could question it. If Peter, John, and James, the pillars of the church at Jerusalem, as well as Paul and Barnabas, the heads of the gentile mission, arrived at a unanimous decision, all consciences might be satisfied and all opposing mouths stopped.

ATTEMPT TO UNSETTLE

154. It fills us with amazement to discover that even this settlement was not final. It would appear that, even at the time when it was made, it was fiercely opposed by some who were present at the meeting where it was discussed; and, although the authority of the apostles determined the official note that was sent to the distant churches, the Christian community at Jerusalem was agitated with storms of angry opposition to it. Nor did the opposition soon die down. On the contrary, it waxed

stronger and stronger. It was fed from abundant sources. Fierce national pride and prejudice sustained it; it was probably nourished by self-interest, because the Jewish Christians would live on easier terms with the non-Christian Jews the less the difference between them was understood to be; religious conviction, rapidly warming into fanaticism, strengthened it; and soon it was reinforced by all the rancor of hatred and the zeal of propagandism. To such a height did this opposition rise that the part that was inflamed with it at length resolved to send out propagandists to visit the gentile churches one by one and, in contradiction to the official apostolic edict, warn them that they were imperiling their souls by omitting circumcision, and could not enjoy the privileges of true Christianity unless they kept the Jewish law.

155. For years and years these emissaries of a narrow-minded fanaticism, which believed itself to be the only genuine Christianity, diffused themselves over all the churches founded by Paul throughout the gentile world. Their work was not to found churches of their own; they had none of the original pioneer ability of their great rival. Their business was to steal into the Christian communities he had founded and win them to their own narrow views. They haunted Paul's footsteps wherever he went, and for many years were a cause of unspeakable pain to him. They whispered to his converts that his version of the gospel was not the true one, and that his authority was not to be trusted. Was he one of the twelve apostles? Had he kept company with Christ? They represented themselves as having brought the true form of Christianity from Jerusalem, the sacred headquarters; and they did not hesitate to profess that they had been sent from the apostles there. They distorted the noblest parts of Paul's conduct to their purpose. For instance, his refusal to accept money for his services they imputed to a sense of his own lack of authority: the real apostles always received pay. In the same way they misconstrued his abstinence from marriage. They were men not without ability for the work they had undertaken: they had smooth, insinuating tongues, they could assume an air of dignity, and they did not stick at trifles.

156. Unfortunately they were by no means without success. They alarmed the consciences of Paul's converts and poisoned their minds against him. The Galatian church especially fell a prey to them; and the Corinthian church allowed its mind to be turned against its founder. But, indeed, the defection was more or less pronounced everywhere. It seemed as if the whole structure that Paul had built with years of labor was to be thrown to the ground. For this was what he believed to be happening. Though these men called themselves Christians, Paul utterly denied their Christianity. Theirs was not another gospel; if his converts believed it, he assured them they were fallen from grace; and in the most solemn terms he pronounced a curse on those who were thus destroying the temple of God he had built.

PAUL CRUSHES THE JUDAIZERS

157. He was not, however, the man to allow such seduction to go on among his converts without putting forth the most strenuous efforts to counteract it. He hurried, when he could, to see the churches that were being tampered with; he sent messengers to bring them back to their allegiance; above all, he wrote letters to those in peril—letters in which the extraordinary powers of his mind were exerted to the utmost. He argued the subject out with all the resources of logic and Scripture; he exposed the seducers with a keenness which cut like steel and overwhelmed them with outbursts of sarcastic wit; he flung himself at his converts' feet and with all the passion and tenderness of his mighty heart implored them to be true to Christ and to himself. We possess the records of these anxieties in our New Testament; and it fills us with gratitude to God and a strange tenderness to Paul himself to think that out of his heartbreaking trial there has come such a precious heritage to us.

158. It is comforting to know that he was successful. Persevering as his enemies were, he was more than a match for them. Hatred is strong, but stronger still is love. In his later writings the traces of his opposition are minimal or entirely absent. It had given way before the crushing force of his polemic, and its traces had been swept off the soil of the church. Had the event been otherwise, Christianity would have been a river lost in the sands of prejudice near its very source; it would have been at the present day a forgotten Jewish sect instead of the religion of the world.

CHRISTIAN JEWS AND THE LAW

159. Up to this point the course of this ancient controversy can be clearly traced. But there is another branch of it whose course is far from easy to arrive at with certainty. What was the relation of the Christian Jews to the Law, according to the teaching and preaching of Paul? Was it their duty to abandon the practices by which they had been regulating their lives and abstaining from circumcising their children or teaching them to keep the Law? This would appear to be implied in Paul's principles. If Gentiles could enter the kingdom without keeping the Law, it could not be necessary for Jews to keep it. If the Law was a severe discipline intended to drive men to Christ, its obligations fell away when this purpose was fulfilled. The bondage of tutelage ceased as soon as the Son entered on the actual possession of His inheritance.

160. It is certain, however, that the other apostles and the mass of the Christians of Jerusalem did not realize this for a long time. The apostles had agreed not to demand from the gentile Christians circumcision and the keeping of the Law. But they kept it themselves and expected all Jews to keep it. This involved a contradiction of ideas, and it led to unhappy practical consequences. If it had continued or been yielded to by Paul, it would have split up the church into two sections, one of which would have looked down on the other, for it was part of the strict observance of the law to refuse to eat with the uncircumcised; and the Jews would have refused to sit at the same table with those whom they acknowledged to be their Christian brethren. This unseemly contradiction actually came to pass in a prominent instance. The apostle Peter, chancing on one occasion to be in the heathen city of Antioch, at first mingled freely in social intercourse with the gentile Christians. But some of the stricter sort, coming there from Jerusalem, so intimidated him that he withdrew from the gentile table and held aloof from his fellow Christians. Even Barnabas was carried away by the same tyranny of bigotry. Paul alone was true to the principles of gospel freedom, withstanding Peter to the face and exposing the inconsistency of his conduct.

161. Paul never carried on a polemic against circumcision and the keeping of the law among born Jews. This was reported of him by his enemies; but it was a false report. When he arrived in Jerusalem at the close of his third missionary journey, the apostle James and the elders informed him of the damage that this representation was doing to his good name and advised him publicly to disprove it. The words in which they made this appeal to him are very remarkable. "Thou seest, brother," they said, "how many thousands of Jews there are who believe; and they are all zealous of the law; and they are informed of thee that thou teachest all the Jews who are among the Gentiles to forsake Moses, saying that they ought not to circumcise their children, neither to walk after the customs. Do therefore this that we say to thee: We have four men who have a vow on them. Take them and purify thyself with them, and be at charges with them, that they may shave their heads; and all may know that those things whereof they were informed concerning thee are nothing, but thou thyself also walkest orderly and keepest the law."

Paul complied with this appeal and went through the rite that James recommended. This clearly proves that he never regarded it as part of his work to dissuade born Jews from living as Jews. It may be thought that he ought to have done so—that his principles required a stern opposition to everything associated with the dispensation that had passed away. He understood them differently, however, and had a good reason to stand for the line he pursued.

We find him advising those who were called into the kingdom of Christ being circumcised not to become uncircumcised, and those called in circumcision not to submit to circumcision; and the reason he gives is that circumcision is nothing and uncircumcision is nothing. The distinction was nothing more to him, in a religious point of view, than the distinction of sex or the distinction of slave and master. In short, it had no religious significance at all. If, however, a man professed Jewish modes of life as a mark of his nationality, Paul had no quarrel with him; indeed, in some degree he preferred them himself. He argued as little against mere forms as for them; only, if they stood between the soul and Christ or between a Christian and his brethren, then he was their uncompromising opponent. But he knew that liberty may be made an instrument of oppression as well as bondage, and therefore, in regard to meats, for instance, he penned those noble recommendations of self-denial for the sake of weak and scrupulous consciences that are among the most touching testimonies to his utter unselfishness.

162. Indeed, we have here a man of such heroic size that it is no easy matter to define him. Along with the clearest vision of the lines of demarcation between the old and the new in the greatest crisis of human history and an unfaltering championship of principle when real issues were involved, we see in him the most genial superiority to mere formal rules and the utmost consideration for the feelings of those who did not see as he saw. By one huge blow he had cut himself free from the bigotry of bondage; but he never fell into the bigotry of liberty, and had always far loftier aims in view than the mere logic of his own position.

10

THE END

RETURN TO JERUSALEM

163. After completing his brief visit to Greece at the close of his third missionary journey, Paul returned to

Jerusalem. He must by this time have been nearly sixty years of age; and for twenty years he had been engaged in almost superhuman labors. He had been traveling and preaching incessantly, and carrying on his heart a crushing weight of cares. His body had been worn with disease and mangled with punishments and abuse; and his hair must have been whitened, and his face furrowed with the lines of age. As yet, however, there were no signs of his body breaking down, and his spirit was still as sharp as ever in its enthusiasm for the service of Christ.

His eye was especially directed to Rome, and, before leaving Greece, he sent word to the Romans that they might expect to see him soon. But, as he was hurrying toward Jerusalem along the shores of Greece and Asia, the signal sounded that his work was nearly done, and the shadow of approaching death fell across his path. In city after city the persons in the Christian communities who were endowed with the gift of prophecy warned him that bonds and imprisonment were awaiting him, and, as he came nearer to the close of his journey, these warnings became more loud and frequent. He felt their solemnity; his was a brave heart, but it was too humble and reverent not to be overawed with the thought of death and judgment. He had several companions with him, but he sought opportunities of being alone. He parted from his converts as a dying man, telling them that they would see his face no more. But, when they urged him to turn back and avoid the threatened danger, he gently pushed aside their loving arms, and said, "What mean ye to weep and to break my heart? for I am ready not to be bound only, but also to die at Jerusalem for the name of the Lord Jesus."

164. We do not know what business he had on hand which so peremptorily demanded his presence in Jerusalem. He had to deliver to the apostles a collection on behalf of their poor saints, which he had been working hard to gather in the gentile churches; and it may have been of importance that he should discharge this service in person. Or he may have been solicitous to procure from the apostles a message for his gentile churches, giving an authoritative contradiction to the insinuations of his enemies as to the unapostolic character of his gospel. At any event there was some imperative call of duty summoning him, and, in spite of the fear of death and the tears of friends, he went forward to his fate.

PAUL'S ARREST

165. It was the feast of Pentecost when he arrived in the city of his fathers, and, as usual at such seasons, Jerusalem was crowded with hundreds of thousands of pilgrim Jews from all parts of the world. Among these there had to be many who had seen him at the work of evangelization in the cities of the heathen and come into contact with him there. Their rage against him had been checked in foreign lands by the interposition of gentile authority; but might they not, if they met with him in the Jewish capital, wreak on him their vengeance with the support of the whole population?

166. This was actually the danger into which he fell. Certain Jews from Ephesus, the principal scene of his labors during his third journey, recognized him in the temple and, crying out that here was the heretic who blasphemed the Jewish nation, law, and temple, brought about him in an instant a raging sea of fanaticism. It is a wonder he was not torn limb from limb on the spot; but superstition prevented his assailants from defiling with blood the court of the Jews, in which he was caught, and, before they got him hustled into the court of the Gentiles, where they would soon have despatched him, the Roman guard, whose sentries were pacing the castle ramparts that over-looked the temple courts, rushed down and took him under their protection; and, when their captain learned that he was a Roman citizen, his safety was secured.

167. But the fanaticism of Jerusalem was now thoroughly aroused, and it raged against the protection that surrounded Paul like an angry sea. The Roman captain on the day after the apprehension took him down to the Sanhedrin in order to consider the charge against him; but the sight of the prisoner created such an uproar that he had to hurry him away, lest he should be torn in pieces. Strange city and strange people! There was never a nation that produced sons more richly endowed with gifts to make her name immortal; there was never a city whose children clung to her with a more passionate affection; yet, like a mad mother, she tore the best of them in pieces and dashed them mangled from her breast. Jerusalem was now within a few years of her destruction; here, the last of her inspired and prophetic sons came to visit her for the last time, with boundless love to her in his heart; but she would have murdered him; and only the shields of the Gentiles saved him from her fury.

168. Forty zealots banded themselves together under a curse to snatch Paul even from the midst of the Roman swords; and the Roman captain was able to foil their plot only by sending him under a heavy escort down to Caesarea. This was a Roman city on the Mediterranean coast; it was the residence of the Roman governor of Palestine and the headquarters of the Roman garrison; and in it the apostle was perfectly safe from Jewish violence.

IMPRISONMENT AT CAESAREA

169. Here he remained in prison for two years. The Jewish authorities attempted again and again either to procure his condemnation by the governor or to get him delivered up to them, to be tried as an ecclesiastical offender; but they failed to convince the governor that Paul had been guilty of any crime he could recognize or to persuade him to hand over a Roman citizen to their tender mercies. The prisoner ought to have been released, but his enemies were so vehement in asserting that he was a criminal of the worst kind that he was detained on the chance of new evidence turning up against him. Besides, his release was prevented by the expectation of the corrupt governor, Felix, that the life of the leader of a religious sect might be purchased from him with a bribe. Felix was interested in his prisoner and even heard him gladly, as Herod had listened to the Baptist.

170. Paul was not kept in close confinement; he had at least the range of the barracks in which he was detained. There we can imagine him pacing the ramparts on the edge of the Mediterranean, and gazing wistfully across the blue waters in the direction of Macedonia, Achaia, and Ephesus, where his spiritual children were longing for him or perhaps encountering dangers in which they sorely needed his presence.

It was a mysterious providence that thus arrested his energies and condemned the ardent worker to inactivity. Yet we can see now the reason for it. Paul needed rest. After twenty years of incessant evangelization he required leisure time to garner the harvest of experience. During all that time he had been preaching that view of the gospel which at the beginning of his Christian career he had thought out, under the influence of the revealing Spirit, in the solitudes of Arabia. But he had now reached a stage when, with time to think, he might penetrate into deeper regions of the truth as it is in Jesus. And it was so important that he should have this, that in order to secure it, God even permitted him to be shut up in prison.

PAUL'S LATER GOSPEL

171. During these two years he wrote nothing; it was a time of internal mental activity and silent progress. But, when he began to write again, the results of it were at once discernible. The Epistles written after this imprisonment have a mellower tone and set forth a more profound view of doctrine than his earlier writings. There is no contradiction, indeed, or inconsistency between his earlier and later views: in Ephesians and Colossians he builds on the broad foundations laid in Romans and Galatians. But the superstructure is loftier and more imposing. He dwells less on the work of Christ and more on His person; less on the justification of the sinner and more on the sanctification of the saint.

In the gospel revealed to him in Arabia he had set Christ forth as dominating mundane history, and shown His first coming to be the point toward which the destinies of Jews and Gentiles had been heading. In the gospel revealed to him at Caesarea the point of view is extra-mundane: Christ is represented as the reason for the creation of all things, and as the Lord of angels and of worlds, to whose second coming the vast procession of the universe is moving toward—of whom, and through whom, and to whom are all things.

In the earlier Epistles the initial act of the Christian life—the justification of the soul—is explained with exhaustive elaboration: but in the later Epistles it is on the subsequent relations to Christ of the person who has been already justified that the apostle chiefly dwells. According to his teaching, the whole spectacle of the Christian life is due to a union between Christ and the soul; and for the description of this relationship he has invented a vocabulary of phrases and illustrations: believers are in Christ, and Christ is in them: they have the same relation to Him as the stones of a building to the foundation stone, as the branches to the tree, as the members to the head, as a wife to her husband. This union is ideal, for the divine mind in eternity made the destiny of Christ and the believer one; it is legal, for their debts and merits are common property; it is vital, for the connection with Christ supplies the power of a holy and progressive life; it is moral, for, in mind and heart, in character and conduct, Christians are constantly becoming more and more like Christ.

HIS ETHICS

172. Another feature of these later Epistles is the balance between their theological and their moral teaching. This is visible even in the external structure of the greatest of them, for they are nearly equally divided into two parts, the first of which is occupied with doctrinal statements and the second with moral exhortations. The ethical teaching of Paul spreads itself over all parts of the Christian life; but it is not distinguished by a systematic arrangement of the various kinds of duties, although the domestic duties are pretty fully treated. Its chief characteristic lies in the motives it brings to bear upon conduct.

To Paul Christian morality was emphatically a morality of motives. The whole history of Christ, not in the details of His earthly life, but in the great features of His redemptive journey from heaven to earth and from earth back to heaven again, as seen from the extra-mundane standpoint of these Epistles, is a series of examples to be copied by Christians in their daily conduct. No duty is too small to illustrate one or other of the principles that inspired the divinest acts of Christ. The commonest acts of humility and beneficence are to be imitations of the condescension that brought Him from the position of equality with God to the obedience of the cross; and the ruling motive of the love and kindness practiced by Christians to one another is to be the recollection of their common connection with Him.

APPEAL TO CAESAR

173. After Paul's imprisonment had lasted for two years, Felix was succeeded in the governorship of Palestine by Festus. The Jews had never ceased to connive to get Paul into their hands, and they at once assailed the new ruler with further demands. As Festus seemed to be wavering, Paul availed himself of his privilege of appeal as a Roman citizen and demanded to be sent to Rome and tried at the bar of the emperor. This could not be refused him; and a prisoner had to be sent to Rome at once after such an appeal was taken. Soon, therefore, Paul was shipped off under the charge of Roman soldiers and in the company of many other prisoners on their way to the same destination.

VOYAGE TO ITALY

174. The journal of the voyage has been preserved in the Acts of the Apostles and is acknowledged to be the most valuable document in existence concerning the seamanship of ancient times. It is also a precious document of Paul's life, for it shows how his character shone out in a novel situation. A ship is a kind of miniature of the world. It is a floating island, in which there are the government and the governed. But the government is, like that of states, liable to sudden social upheavals, in which the ablest man is thrown to the top. This was a voyage of extreme perils, which required the utmost presence of mind and power of winning the confidence and obedience of those on board. Before it was ended Paul was virtually both the captain of the ship and the general of the soldiers; and all on board owed their lives to him.

ARRIVAL IN ROME

175. At length the dangers of the deep were left behind; and Paul found himself approaching the capital of the Roman world by the Appian Road, the great highway by which Rome was entered by travelers from the East. The bustle and noise increased as he neared the city, and the signs of Roman grandeur and renown multiplied at every step. For many years he had been looking forward to seeing Rome, but he had always thought of entering it in a very different guise from that which he now wore. He had always thought of Rome as a successful general thinks of the central stronghold of the country he is subduing, who eagerly looks forward to the day when he will direct the charge against its gates. Paul was engaged in the conquest of the world for Christ, and Rome was the final position he had hoped to carry in his Master's name. Years ago he had sent to it the famous challenge, "I am ready to preach the gospel to you that are at Rome also; for I am not ashamed of the gospel of Christ, for it is the power of God unto salvation to every one that believeth." But now, when he found himself actually at its gates and thought of the abject conditon in which he was—an old, gray-haired, broken man, a chained prisoner just escaped from shipwreck—his heart sank within him, and he felt dreadfully alone.

At the right moment, however, a little incident took place that restored him to himself: at a small town forty miles out of Rome he was met by a little band of Christian brethren, who, hearing of his approach, had come out to welcome him; and, ten miles farther on, he came upon another group, who had come out for the same purpose. Self-reliant as he was, he was exceedingly sensitive to human sympathy, and the sight of these brethren and their interest in him completely revived him. He thanked God and took courage; his old feelings came back in their accustomed strength; and, when, in the company of these friends, he reached that shoulder of the Alban Hills from which the first view of the city is seen, his heart swelled with the anticipation of victory, for he knew he carried in his breast the force that would yet lead captive that proud capital.

It was not with the step of a prisoner, but with that of a conqueror, that he passed at length beneath the city gate. His road lay along that very Sacred Way by which many a Roman general had passed in triumph to the capital, seated on a car of victory, followed by the prisoners and spoils of the enemy, and surrounded with the plaudits of rejoicing Rome. Paul looked little like such a hero: no car of victory carried him, he walked the highway with wayworn foot; no medals or ornaments adorned his person, a chain of iron dangled from his wrist; no applauding crowds welcomed his approach, a few humble friends formed all his escort; yet never did a more truly conquering footstep fall on the pavement of Rome or a heart more confident of victory pass within her gates.

IMPRISONMENT

176. Meanwhile, however, it was not to the capital his steps were bent, but to a prison; and he was destined to lie in prison long, for his trial did not come up for two years. The law's delays have been proverbial in all countries and at all eras; and the law of imperial Rome was not likely to be free from this reproach during the reign of Nero, a man of such frivolity that any engagement of pleasure was sufficient to make him put off the most important call of business. The imprisonment, it is true, was of the mildest description. It may have been that the officer who brought him to Rome spoke a good word for the man who had saved his life during the voyage, or the officer to whom he was handed over, and who is known in profane history as a man of justice and humanity, may have inquired into his case and formed a favorable opinion of his character; but at any event Paul was permitted to rent a house of his own and live in it in perfect freedom, with the single exception that a soldier, who was responsible for his person, was his constant attendant.

OCCUPATION IN PRISON

177. This was far from the condition that such an active spirit would have coveted. He would have liked to be moving from synagogue to synagogue in the immense city, preaching in its streets and squares, and founding congregation after congregation among the masses of its population. Another man, arrested for a similar time of ceaseless movement and held within prison walls, might have allowed his mind to stagnate in sloth and despair. But Paul behaved differently. Availing himself of every possibility of the situation, he converted his one room into a center of far-reaching activity and beneficence. On the few square feet of space allowed him he erected a fulcrum with which he moved the world, establishing within the walls of Nero's capital a sovereignty more extensive than his own.

178. Even the most irksome circumstance of his lot was turned to good measure. This was the soldier by whom he was watched. To a man of Paul's eager temperament and restlessness of mood this must often have been an intolerable annoyance; and, indeed, in the letters written during this imprisonment he is constantly referring to his chain, as if it were never out of his mind. But he did not suffer this irritation to blind him to the opportunity of doing good presented by the situation. Of course his attendant was changed every few hours, as one soldier relieved another on guard. In this way there might be six or eight with him twenty-four hours. They belonged to the imperial guard, the flower of the Roman army.

Paul could not sit for hours beside another man without speaking of the subject that lay nearest his heart. He spoke to these soldiers about their immortal souls and the faith of Christ. To men accustomed to the horrors of Roman warfare and the manners of Roman barracks nothing could be more striking than a life and character like his; and the result of these conversations was that many of them became changed men, and a revival spread through the barracks and penetrated into the imperial household itself. His room was sometimes crowded with these stern, bronzed faces, glad to see him at other times than those when duty required them to be there. He sympathized with them and entered into the spirit of their occupation; indeed, he was full of the spirit of the warrior himself.

We have an imperishable relic of these visits in an outburst of inspired eloquence that he dictated at this period: "Put on the whole armor of God, that ye may be able to stand against the wiles of the devil; for we wrestle not against flesh and blood, but against principalities, against powers, against the rulers of the darkness of this world, against spiritual wickedness in high places. Wherefore take unto you the whole armor of God, that ye may be able to withstand in the evil day and, having done all, to stand. Stand therefore, having your loins girt about with truth, and having on the breastplate of righteousness, and your feet shod with the preparation of the gospel of peace; above all, taking the shield of faith, wherewith ye shall be able to quench all the fiery darts of the wicked. And take the helmet of salvation and the sword of the Spirit, which is the word of God." That picture was drawn from the life, from the armor of the soldiers in his room; and perhaps these ringing sentences were first poured into the ears of his warlike auditors before they were transferred to the epistle in which they have been preserved.

VISITORS

179. But he had other visitors. All who took an interest in Christianity in Rome, both Jews and Gentiles, came to him. Perhaps there was not a day of the two years of his imprisonment but he had such visitors. The Roman Christians learned to go to that room as to an oracle or shrine. Many a Christian teacher had his sword sharpened there; and new energy began to diffuse itself through the Christian circles of the city. Many an anxious father brought his son, many a friend his friend, hoping that a word from the apostle's lips might waken the sleeping conscience. Many a wanderer, stumbling in there by chance, came out a new man. Such a person was Onesimus, a slave from Colossae, who arrived in Rome as a runaway, but was sent back to his Christian master, Philemon, no longer as a slave, but as a brother beloved.

180. Still more interesting visitors came. At all periods of his life he exercised a strong fascination over young men. They were attracted by the manly soul within him, in which they found sympathy with their aspirations and inspiration for the noblest work. These youthful friends, who were scattered over the world in the work of Christ, flocked to him at Rome. Timothy and Luke, Mark and Aristarchus, Tychicus and Epaphras, and many more came, to drink afresh at the well of his ever-springing wisdom and earnestness. And he sent them forth again, to carry messages to his churches or bring him news of their condition.

181. Of his spiritual children in the distance he never ceased to think. Daily he wandered in imagination among the glens of Galatia and along the shores of Asia and Greece; every night he prayed for the Christians of Antioch and Ephesus, of Philippi and Thessalonica and Corinth. Nor were gratifying proofs that they were remembering him missing. Now and then there would appear in his lodging a deputy from some distant church, bringing the greetings of his converts or, perhaps, a contribution to meet his temporal wants, or desiring his decision on some point of doctrine or practice about which difficulty had arisen. These messengers were not sent away empty: they carried warmhearted messages of golden words of counsel from their apostolic friend.

Some of them carried far more. When Epaphroditus, a deputy from the church at Philippi, which had sent to their dear father in Christ an offering of love, was returning home, Paul sent with him, in acknowledgment of their kindness, the Epistle to the Philippians, the most beautiful of all his letters, in which he lays bare his very heart and every sentence glows with love more tender than a woman's. When the slave Onesimus was sent back to Colossae, he received, as the branch of peace to offer to his master, the exquisite little Epistle to Philemon, a priceless monument of Christian courtesy. He carried, too, a letter addressed to the church of the town in which his master lived, the Epistle to the Colossians.

The composition of these Epistles was by far the most important part of Paul's varied prison activity; and he crowned this labor with the writing of the Epistle to the Ephesians, which is perhaps the profoundest and sublimest book in the world. The church of Christ has derived many benefits from the imprisonment of the servants of God; the greatest book of uninspired religious genius, Pilgrim's Progress, was written in a jail; but never did there come to the church a greater mercy in the disguise of misfortune than when the arrest of Paul's bodily activities at Caesarea and Rome supplied him with the time needed to reach the depths of truth sounded in the Epistle to the Ephesians.

HIS WRITINGS

182. It may have seemed a dark dispensation of providence to Paul himself that the course of life he had pursued so long was so completely changed; but God's thoughts are higher than man's thoughts and His ways than man's ways; and He gave Paul grace to overcome the temptations of his situation and do far more in his enforced inactivity for the welfare of the world and the permanence of his own influence than he could have done by twenty years of wandering missionary work. Sitting in his room, he gathered within the sounding cavity of his sympathetic heart the sighs and cries of thousands far away, and diffused courage and help in every direction from his own inexhaustible resources. He sank his mind deeper and deeper in solitary thought, until, smiting the rock in the dim depth to which he had descended, he caused streams to gush forth that are still gladdening the city of God.

RELEASE FROM PRISON

183. The Book of Acts suddenly breaks off with a brief summary of Paul's two years' imprisonment at Rome. Is this because there was no more to tell? When his trial came, did it result in his condemnation and death? Or did he get out of prison and resume his old occupations? Where Luke's lucid narrative so suddenly deserts us, tradition comes in proffering its doubtful aid. It tells us that he was acquitted on his trial and let out of prison; that he resumed his travels, visiting Spain among other places; but that before long he was arrested again and sent back to Rome, where he died a martyr's death at the cruel hands of Nero.

NEW JOURNEYS

184. Happily, however, we are not altogether dependent on the precarious aid of tradition. We have writings of Paul's own undoubtedly subsequent to the two years of his first imprisonment. These are what are called the Pastoral Epistles—the Epistles to Timothy and Titus. In these we see that he regained his liberty and resumed his employment of revisiting his old churches and founding new ones. His footsteps cannot, indeed, be any longer traced with certainty. We find him back at Ephesus and Troas; we find him in Crete, an island where he touched on his voyage to Rome and in which he may then have become interested; we find him exploring new territory in the northern parts of Greece. We see him once more, like the commander of an army who sends his aides-de-camp all over the field of battle, sending out his young assistants to organize and watch over the churches.

185. But this was not to last long. An event had happened immediately after his release from prison that could not but influence his fate. This was the burning of Rome—an appalling disaster, the glare of which even at this distance makes the heart shudder. It was probably a mad freak of the malicious monster who then wore the imperial purple. But Nero saw fit to attribute it to the Christians, and instantly the most atrocious persecution broke out against them. Of course the fame of this soon spread over the Roman world; and it was not likely that the foremost apostle of Christianity could long escape. Every Roman governor knew that he could not do the emperor a more pleasing service than by sending to him Paul in chains.

SECOND IMPRISONMENT

186. It was not long, accordingly, before Paul was lying once more in prison at Rome; and it was no mild imprisonment this time, but the worst known to the law. No troops of friends now filled his room, for the Christians of Rome had been massacred or scattered, and it was dangerous for any one to claim himself a Christian. We have a letter written from his dungeon, the last he ever wrote, the Second Epistle to Timothy, which affords us a glimpse of unspeakable pathos into the circumstances of the prisoner. He tells us that one part of his trial is already over. Not a friend stood by him as he faced the blood-thirsty tyrant who sat on the judgment seat. But the Lord stood by him and enabled him to make the emperor and the spectators in the crowded basilica hear the sound of the gospel. The charge against him had broken down. But he had no hope of escape. Other stages of the trial had yet to come, and he knew that evidence to condemn him would either be discovered or manufactured.

The letter betrays the miseries of his dungeon. He asks Timothy to bring a cloak he had left at Troas, to defend him from the damp of the cell and the cold of the winter. He asks for his books and parchments, that he may relieve the tedium of his solitary hours with the studies he had always loved. But, above all, he beseeches Timothy to come himself, for he was longing to feel the touch of a friendly hand and see the face of a friend yet once again before he died.

Was the brave heart then conquered at last? Read the Epistle and see. How does it begin? "I also suffer these things; nevertheless I am not ashamed; for I know whom I have believed, and am persuaded that he is able to keep that which I have committed unto him against that day." How does it end? "I am now ready to be offered, and the time of my departure is at hand. I have fought a good fight, I have finished my course, I have kept the faith. Henceforth there is laid up for me a crown of righteousness, which the Lord, the righteous judge, shall give me at that day; and not to me only, but unto all them that love his appearing." That is not the strain of the vanquished.

TRIAL

187. There can be little doubt that he appeared again at Nero's bar, and this time the charge did not break down. In all history there is not a more startling illustration of the irony of human life than this scene of Paul at the bar of Nero. On the judgment seat, clad in the imperial purple, sat a man who in a bad world had attained the eminence of being the very worst and meanest person in it—a man stained with every crime, the murder of his own mother, of his wives, and of his best benefactors; a man whose whole being was so steeped in every namable and unamable vice that his body and soul were, as someone said at the time, nothing but a compound of mud and blood; and in the prisoner's dock stood the best man the world contained, his hair whitened with labors for the good of men and the glory of God. Such was the occupant of the seat of justice, and such the man who stood in the place of the criminal.

DEATH

188. The trial ended, Paul was condemned and delivered to the executioner. He was led out of the city with a crowd of the lowest rabble at his heels. The fatal spot was reached; he knelt beside the block; the headsman's axe gleamed in the sun and fell; and the head of the apostle of the world rolled down in the dust.

189. So sin did its uttermost and its worst. Yet how poor and empty was its triumph! The blow of the axe only cut off the lock of the prison and let the spirit go forth to its home and to its crown. The city falsely called eternal dismissed him with execration from her gates; but ten thousand times ten thousand welcomed him in the same hour at the gates of the city that is really eternal. Even on earth Paul could not die. He lives among us today with a life one hundred times more influential than that which throbbed in his brain while the earthly form that made him visible still lingered on the earth. Wherever the feet of those who publish the glad tidings go forth beautiful on the mountains, he walks by their side as an inspirer and a guide; in ten thousand churches every Sunday and on a thousand thousand hearths every day his eloquent lips still teach that gospel of which he was never ashamed; and, wherever there are human souls searching for the white flower of holiness of climbing the difficult heights of self-denial, there he whose life was so pure, whose devotion to Christ was so entire, and whose pursuit of a single purpose was so unceasing, is welcomed as the best of friends.

HINTS TO TEACHERS AND QUESTIONS FOR PUPILS

TEACHER'S APPARATUS

English theology has no more just cause for pride than the books it has produced on the life of Paul. Perhaps there is no other subject in which it has so outdistanced all rivals. Conybeare and Howson's *Life and Epistles of St. Paul* will probably always be the best; in many respects it is nearly perfect; and a teacher who has mastered it will be sufficiently equipped for his work and require no other help. The works of Lewin and Farrar are written on the same lines; the former is rich in maps of countries and plans of towns; and the strong point of the latter is the analysis of Paul's writings—the exposition of the mind of Paul. Sir William Ramsay has made the whole subject peculiarly his own by the enthusiasm and labors of a lifetime. The German books are not nearly so valuable. Hausrath's *The Apostle Paul* is a brilliant performance, but it is as weak in handling the deeper things as it is strong in coloring up the external and picturesque features of the subject. Baur's work is an amazingly clever *tour de force,* but it is not so much a well-proportioned picture of the apostle as a prolonged paradox thrown down as a challenge to the learned. The latest large German work, Clemen's *Paulus,* proceeds on the principle that the miracle is untrue, and the effect may be sufficiently seen in the account it gives of the first visit to Philippi. In Weinal's *Paulus,* pp. 312, 313, there appears a forbidding picture of the effects produced by the teaching of the subject in the author's country; in our country, on the contrary, it has long been among the most attractive subjects for both teachers and students. Adolphe Monod's *Saint Paul*, a series of five discourses, is an inquiry into the secret of the apostle's life, written with deep sympathy and glowing eloquence; and Renan's work, with the same title, gives, with unrivaled brilliance, a picture of the world in which the apostle lived, if not of the apostle himself. There are books on the subject that do honor to American scholarship from the pens of Cone, Gilbert, Bacon and A. T. Robertson, the last mentioned with a valuable bibliography. But the best help is to be found in the original sources themselves—the cameolike pictures of Luke and the self-revelations of Paul's Epistles. The latter especially, read in the fresh translation of Conybeare, will show the apostle to anyone who has eyes to see.

CHAPTER 1

Paragraph 2. Subject of class essay—Paul and the other apostles: points of connection and contrast.

5. Subject of class essay—Relation of Christianity to learning and intellectual gifts: its use of them and its independence of them.

9. Quote passages of Scripture in which Paul's destination to be the missionary of the Gentiles is expressed.

CHAPTER 2

On the external features of the period embraced in this chapter compare the corresponding pages of Hausrath; on the internal features see Principal Rainy's lecture on Paul in *The Evangelical Succession Lectures*, vol. i.

14. On the chronology of Paul's life see the notes at the end of Conybeare and Howson, and Farrar, ii. 623.

The principal dates may be given at this stage from Conybeare and Howson, for reference throughout:

A.D.

36. Conversion.
38. Flight to Tarsus.
44. Brought to Antioch by Barnabas.
48. First Missionary Journey.
50. Council at Jerusalem.
51–54. Second Missionary Journey. 1 and 2 *Thessalonians* written at Corinth.
54–58. Third Missionary Journey.
57. *1 Corinthians* written at Ephesus; *2 Corinthians*, in Macedonia; *Galatians*, at Corinth.
58. *Romans* written at Corinth.
    Arrest at Jerusalem.
59. In prison at Caesarea.
60. Voyage to Rome.
62. *Philemon, Colossians, Ephesians, Philippians*, written at Rome.
63. Release from prison.
67. *1 Timothy* and *Titus* written.
68. In prison again at Rome. *2 Timothy*.
    Death.

With these may be compared some of Ramsay's dates—the conversion, 33; First Missionary Journey, 47–49; Second, 50–53; Third, 53–57; Voyage to Rome, 59, 60; Trial and Acquittal, 61; Second Trial, 67.

Whereas Conybeare and Howson consider Galatians to have been written, in close conjunction with Romans, at Corinth during a fourth missionary journey, Ramsay believes it to have been written at Antioch before this journey began; and, whereas the older authorities suppose it to be addressed to Galatians evangelized by Paul during the Second Missionary Journey, though no details of such a conquest are found in Acts, Ramsay holds the recipients of the Epistle to have been the churches in the interior of Asia Minor evangelized during the First Missionary Journey, the regions of Phrygia and Lycaonia in which these were situated forming at that time part of the province of Galatia, the boundaries of which had been extended. This is the South Galatian theory, the fullest statement and defense of which will be found in Hastings' *Dictionary of the Bible*, vol. v.

15. The goat's-hair cloth was called "cilicium," from the name of the province.

16. Dean Howson's *Metaphors of St. Paul*. Also Hausrath, p. 15.

18. Compare the long lists of sins frequent in the Epistle.

23. Subject for class essay: Paul's first sight of Jerusalem.

27. A startling picture of the state of society in Jerusalem might be constructed from the materials supplied in Matthew 23.

28. Detailed comparison of the experience of Paul with that of Luther: their early religious ideas; the state of religion around them; their failure to find peace and their sufferings of conscience; their discovery of the righteousness of God.

On the religious associations of Paul's early life see the first 100 pages of Reuss' *Christian Theology in the Apostolic Age*.

31. On the history of Christianity between the death of Christ and the conversion of St. Paul see Dykes' *From Jerusalem to Antioch*.

34. The question whether Paul was married. His views on the place of woman.

35. Perhaps Acts 26:11 may not imply that any of the Christians yielded to his endeavors to make them blaspheme.

15. What was the Latin name for a town enjoying the political privileges possessed by Tarsus?
16. What are Paul's principal metaphors?
17. Where does he make this boast?
19. What was the Latin name for the Roman citizenship, and what privileges did it include? On what occasions is Paul recorded to have used it? On what occasions might he have been expected to use it, when he omitted to do so? What reasons may be given for the omission?
20. Name friends of Paul who were engaged in the same trade as he.
21. Give Paul's quotations from the Greek poets. Do you know the authors he quoted from? Explain *Septuagint* and *Diaspora.*
22. Where does Paul refer to the sophists and rhetoricians?
26. Make a collection of Paul's quotations from the Old Testament, showing where each of them was taken from.
28. What does Paul mean by the Law?
32. Trace out the points of contact between the language and views of Stephen's speech and those of Paul.
34. Where is it said that Paul voted in the Sanhedrin?
45. Collect Paul's references to the persecution and bring out how severe it was.

CHAPTER 3

On Paul's mental processes before and at the time of his conversion see Principal Rainy's lecture, already quoted.

The conversion of Paul is one of the strong apologetic

positions of Christianity. See this worked out in Lyttelton's *Conversion of St. Paul*. But it might be worked out afresh on more modern lines.

40. Principal Rainy, in the lecture referred to above, says that he sees no evidence of such a conflict as this in Paul's mind; but what, then, is the meaning of "It is hard for thee to kick against the pricks"?

41. The general tenor of the earliest Christian apologetic, as it is to be found in the speeches of the Acts of the Apostles.

44. Nothing could be more alien to the spirit of the New Testament than to turn this around the other way, and, assuming that what Paul saw was only a vision, argue that the other appearances of Christ, because they are put on the same level, may have been only visions too. This is a mere stroke of dilectical cleverness, which shows no regard to the obvious intention of the writers.

> There are three accounts of the conversion of Paul in the Acts. What is the significance of this reduplication in so small a book? Enumerate the differences between these accounts, and explain them.
>
> 38. Prove that the first Christians called Christianity THE WAY, and explain the signification of this name.

CHAPTER 4

On the subject of this chapter see the works on Pauline Theology by Pfleiderer, Bruce, Du Bose, Titius, and Stevens, also the relevant portions of any of the Handbooks of New Testament Theology—Weiss, Reuss, Schmid, van Oosterzee, Beyschlag, Holtzmann, and Stevens. Weiss' exposition is among the most solid and trustworthy. He divides Paulinism into four sections:

I. THE EARLIEST GOSPEL OF PAUL DURING THE HEATHEN MISSION (gathered from Thessalonians). One chapter—The Gospel as the Way of Deliverance from Judgment.

II. THE DOCTRINAL SYSTEM OF THE FOUR GREAT DOCTRINAL AND CONTROVERSIAL EPISTLES (Corinthians, Romans, Galatians). Ch. 1. Universal Sinfulness of Man; ch. 2. Heathenism and Judaism; ch. 3. Prophecy and Fulfillment; ch. 4. Christology; ch. 5. Redemption and Justification; ch. 6. The New Life; ch. 7. The Doctrine of Predestination; ch. 8. The Doctrine of the Church; ch. 9. The Last Things.

III. THE DEVELOPMENT OF THE DOCTRINE IN THE EPISTLES WRITTEN IN PRISON (Colossians, Ephesians, Philippians, Philemon). Ch. 1. The Pauline Foundations; ch. 2. Further Development of Doctrine.

IV. THE TEACHING OF THE PASTORAL EPISTLES. One chapter —Christianity as Doctrine.

51. Subject for class essay: The Sources of St. Paul's Theology.

52. Luther in the Wartburg.

54–65. As these paragraphs are nothing but a paraphrase of Romans 1–8, pupils ought to be asked to compare them to the corresponding paragraphs of the Epistle.

56. Compare Tholuck, *The Moral Character of Heathendom.*

65. On Paul's Psychology see the monograph of Simon and the Handbooks of Biblical Psychology by Delitzsch and Beck: also Heard, *The Tripartite Nature of Man,* Laidlaw, *The Bible Doctrine of Man,* and Dickson, *St. Paul's Use of the Terms Flesh and Spirit.*

67. Compare Somerville, *St. Paul's Conception of Christ,* and Knowling, *The Testimony of St. Paul to Christ.*

51. Where does Paul mention his journey to Arabia?
56. What is the connection between moral and intellectual degeneracy?
62. Where does Paul speak of the Gospel as a "mystery," and what does he mean by this word?
65. Does Paul divide human nature into two or into
three sections? Do you know the theological
names for these alternatives? Does Paul regard the
unregenerate man as possessing the part of
human nature which he calls "spirit"?
67. Enumerate the incidents of Christ's earthly life
referred to by Paul.

CHAPTER 5

On this subject see the first two chapters of Cony-
beare and Howson; *New Testament Times* of Hausrath or
Schürer; Fairweather, *From the Exile to the Advent*, Moss,
From Malachi to Matthew.

72. Subject of class essay: The Origin and
Significance of the name "Christian."

72. By what other names were the Christians called in
New Testament times, among themselves or
among their enemies?
78. What did the Greeks, the Romans, and the Jews
severally contribute to Christianity?

CHAPTER 6

The aim of this handbook, as of *The Life of Jesus Christ*
in the same series, being to show at a single glance the
general course of the life and the principal objects it
touched, a good many details have been omitted. This is
especially the case in this chapter and in chapter 10. The
omissions cause those great features to stand out more
prominently which details are apt to obscure. In this
chapter an endeavor has been made to show in this way

what were the different regions into which the apostle traveled, and what the peculiarities and the extent of the work he did in each. But in an extended Bible class course the lessons will naturally go more into detail, and perhaps the incidents that took place in each town may generally form a lesson. Here, therefore, and at the beginning of chapter 10, a few hints may be given of the viewpoints for the lessons, insofar as these are not already supplied in the text.

Acts

13:1–12. First Footsteps of Christian Missions.
13:14–52. *Antioch.* Paul's Missionary Method.
14:1–6. *Iconium.* Among the Jews.
14:6–20. *Lystra.* Among the Heathens.
14:21–28. Paul as a Pastor.
15: Paul as an Ecclesiastic.
16:1–6. The New Companion.
16:6–10. Opening up Virgin Soil.
16:12–40. *Philippi.* Transfiguration and Disfiguration of Humanity.
17:1–9. *Thessalonica.* An Honorable Reproach.
17:10–14. *Beroea.* Rare Freedom from Prejudice.
17:15–34. *Athens.* The Gospel and Intellectual Curiosity.
18:1–3. *Corinth.* Paul's Earthly Home.
18:4–17. The Missionary's Discouragements and Encouragements.
18:23–28. A polished Shaft in God's Quiver.
19: *Ephesus.* See the text. Also, Conflict of Christianity with Vested Interests and Mob Violence.

79. Howson's *Companions of St. Paul.*

81. A minute inspection of Acts 13:9 will confirm the view given here of the change of name, though it is difficult to get rid of the idea that the conversion of the governor, who bore the same name, had something to do with it.

84. On the worship of the synagogue see Farrar's *Life of Christ*, i. 220.

89. On the Council of Jerusalem, which took place between the first and second journeys, see chapter 9.

93. What is said here of the plan of the Acts explains still more strikingly the meagerness of the record of the third journey.

97. Beroea was to the south of the Via Egnatia.

99. Subject of class essay: The Influence of Christianity on the Lot of Woman.

103. Subject of class essay: Paul at Athens.

104. Subject of class essay: Paul and Socrates.

113. A strong argument against the mythical theory of the miracles of our Lord may be constructed from the paucity of the miracles attributed to Paul. If that age naturally wove miraculous legends around great names, why did it not encircle Paul with a continuous web of miracle? And why does the New Testament admit that the Baptist worked no miracle?

114. See Ramsay, *Letters to the Seven Churches.*

79. Give a list of Paul's companions and friends mentioned in the New Testament.
84. What were the charges generally brought against him before the authorities?
91. Where in his writings does he mention Barnabas and Mark?
93. Give the places in Acts where the items of this catalog are recorded.
94. Mention other classical associations of this region.

98. What two kings of Macedonia are famous in history?
102. Expand these allusions to Greek history.
103. Give a number of the names associated with the golden age of Athens and mention what they were famous for.
108. Find out all the visions mentioned in Paul's life, and prove that they were given him at the crises of his history.
110. Distinguish our Asia and Asia Minor from the Asia of the New Testament.

CHAPTER 7

In the chronological table, the dates of the Epistles have already been given and the points of the history indicated where they come in. It is a pity the Epistles are not arranged in chronological order in our Bibles. Their characteristics may be mentioned:

1 and 2 *Thessalonians.* Simple beginnings. Attitude to Christ's second coming.
1 *Corinthians.* Picture of an apostolic church.
2 *Corinthians.* Paul's portrait of himself.
Galatians. Vehement polemic against Judaizers.
Romans. Paul's gospel.
Philemon. Example of Christian courtesy.
Colossians and *Ephesians.* Paul's later gospel.
Philippians. Picture of Roman imprisonment.
1 *Timothy* and *Titus.* Form of the church.
2 *Timothy.* The last scenes.

Ramsay places *Galatians* before 1 and 2 *Corinthians.*

116. Compare Shaw, *The Pauline Epistles.*

118. On Paul's style see Farrar's Excursus at the close of vol. i. The comparison of it to that of Thucydides is more dignified than that of the text, but less true.

119. Inspiration did not interfere with natural characteristics of style. It made the writer not less but more himself, while of course it imparted to the products of his pen a divine value and authority.

120–127. Howson's *Character of St. Paul*; Speer, *The Man Paul*; Hausrath, 45–57; Baur's remarks (ii. 294ff.) on his intellectual character are very good. But the principal sources are 2 Corinthians and Acts 20.

122. Farrar's treatment of Paul's bodily infirmities is a serious blot on his book, for these are obtruded with a frequency and exaggeration that produce an impression quite different from that made by the references to them in Scripture. This is still truer of Baring-Gould's *Study of St. Paul*. For a treatment of the same subject, realistic, but full of sympathy and delicacy, see Monod. Ramsay is of the opinion that the "thorn in the flesh" was chronic malarial fever.

> 122ff. Illustrate these paragraphs fully from Scripture.
> 123. Compare Paul with Livingstone and other missionaries.

CHAPTER 8

On this subject compare Neander's *Planting of Christianity*, Book ii., ch. 7, and Schaff's *Church History*; also Bannerman's *Church of Christ*. This chapter is only a piecing together of the information scattered through 1 Corinthians. It would be well to get pupils to seek out the passages of the Epistle that correspond to the different paragraphs. A picture of a Pauline church of a later date might be compiled in the same way from the Pastoral Epistles.

136. The doctrine of the Holy Spirit was revealed "at sundry times and in divers manners," and the complete doctrine is to be obtained by uniting the representations of the various writers of Scripture. In the New Testament there are four phrases: 1) In the Synoptic Gospels the Holy Spirit is set forth in His influence on the human nature of Christ; 2) in the Acts and Paul, as the power for founding the church and converting the world; 3) in Paul as the principle of the new life of Christians; 4) in John as the Comforter.

138. Compare the irregularities of other periods of vast change, e.g., the Reformation.

144. On the extent to which an authoritative ecclesiastical system is given in the New Testament compare *Jus Divinum Presbyterii* and Hooker's *Ecclesiastical Polity*.

> 130. Give the names of the principal games of ancient times, derived from the places where they were held.
> 131. Where are churches mentioned as meeting in the houses of individuals?
> 132. Explain the words "barbarian," "Scythian," in Col. 3:11.
> 135. What modern divine endeavored to revive these phenomena, and what is the name of the church he founded? What is the meaning of the word "charism"? Were the tongues of Pentecost the same as those of 1 Corinthians? Give instances in which New Testament prophets did predict future events.

CHAPTER 9

The criticism that seeks to distintegrate the New Testament writings and set the apostles against one another is founded on a revival of the claim of the Judaizers that their propaganda had the sanction of Peter and the other original apostles. In a handbook like this it is impossible to discuss at any length the Tübingen Theory. But some of its points are silently met in the text; and the whole theory is answered by an attempt to give a view of the course of the controversy that covers all the facts. The distinction drawn in paragraphs 159ff. between the central question in dispute and a subordinate aspect of the controversy will be found to clear up many intricacies. Compare Sorley's *Jewish Christians and Judaism.*

This chapter is full of references to passages in Acts and Galatians, which pupils ought to be asked to produce.

CHAPTER 10

Viewpoints for lessons on details omitted or only slightly referred to in the text:

Acts
20:4–16. Paul the Hirer of Laborers for Christ's Vineyard: the Unwearied Preacher *(Troas).*
20:17–38. The Man of Heart *(Miletus).*
22: Final Effort to save his country.
23:1–10. In the Dock where he had placed others.
23:22–27. The Preacher of Righteousness.
26: The Inspired Student.
27: Paul as a Ruler of Men.
28: The benevolence of Nature and that of Grace *(Malta).*

171. See notes on chapter 4.

The authenticity of Ephesians and Colossians can be denied only by ignoring the impression of majesty and profundity that they have made on the greatest minds. (See the Introductions in Meyer and Alford.) What other mind of those ages except Paul's could have erected a structure so magnificent on the very foundations of the Epistle to the Romans? Or in what other mind was there such a union of the doctrinal and the ethical?

In John's writings the relation of believers to Christ is illustrated by a far higher comparison: it is compared to the union of Father and Son in the Deity.

172. See Ernesti: *The Ethic of Paul;* also Juncker.

174. See Smith's *Voyage of St. Paul;* also Sir William Ramsay's article on Roads and Travel in Hastings' *Dictionary of the Bible,* vol. v.

176. Burrus, the Praetorian Prefect. So Conybeare and Howson; but Ramsay, following Mommsen, holds the officer to have been the princeps peregrinorum, whose quarters lay on the Coelian Hill.

On the various kinds of imprisonment in Roman law see Ramsay's *Roman Antiquities,* ch. ix.

177–182. The materials for this account of Paul's prison life at Rome are chiefly gathered from the Epistle to the Philippians.

184. On the genuineness of the Pastoral Epistles see essay by Findley in Sabatier's *The Apostle Paul.* The comparative lack of doctrinal matter in them is accounted for by the fact that they were written to ministers well acquainted with his doctrinal system.

188. At Tre Fontane, to the south of Rome, the traditional scene of the execution is still pointed out; and not far off stands St. Paul's-outside-the-Walls, one of the most gorgeous churches in the world.

164. Trace the different collections that Paul is recorded to have been engaged with.
166. What were the courts of the temple; and what was the name of the Roman fortress that overlooked them?

171. How often does the phrase "in Christ" (or "in" with pronouns referring to Christ) occur in Ephesians?
172. Give examples from Paul's writings of the application of great principles to small duties.
175. Give the names and localities of other great Roman roads. Describe a Roman triumph.
179. Narrate the story of Onesimus, gathering it from the Epistle to Philemon.
184. Explain the name of the Pastoral Epistles.